Discovering Musicianship

Grade One

by James Thomas

PASCAL
PRESS

Copyright © 1999 James Thomas

ISBN 1 74020 026 8

Pascal Press
PO Box 250
Glebe NSW 2037
(02) 9557 4844
http://www.pascalpress.com.au

Typeset by Ragland Park Productions
Printed in Australia by McPherson's Printing Group

Acknowledgements

Special thanks to all those who helped in the production of this book including reviewers and proofreaders, the librarians at the Janáček Academy of Performing Arts (Brno), Jane Scheider, Tom Samek, Karl Vyzard, Šarka Pelanová, Michelle Patane and Diana Grivas.

Sadie, S. (ed.) 1980, *The New Grove Dictionary of Music and Musicians*, Macmillan Publishers Ltd, London.
Barlow, H. & Morgenstern, S. (eds.) 1983, *A Dictionary of Musical Themes*, Faber, London.
Brandon, H. (ed.) 1969, *Fifty Folk Songs*, Allans Edition, Australia.
Thanks to Curtiss Brown Ltd/United Music Publishers for permission to use an extract from Ogden Nash's *Carnival of the Animals*.

Apart from any fair dealing for the purposes of study, research, criticism or review, as permitted under the Copyright Act, no part may be reproduced by any process without written permission. Inquiries should be made to the publisher.

Contents

Introduction	**iv**
Unit One	**1**
Revision Worksheet One	**10**
Unit Two	**11**
Revision Worksheet Two	**22**
Unit Three	**26**
Revision Worksheet Three	**36**
Unit Four	**39**
Revision Worksheet Four	**49**
Unit Five	**51**
Revision Worksheet Five	**60**
Unit Six	**64**
Revision Worksheet Six	**75**
Unit Seven	**79**
Revision Worksheet Seven	**87**
Glossary	**89**
Answer Section	**92**

Introduction

♪ To the Teacher

Discovering Musicianship serves younger and older students beginning their theoretical studies in music. For younger students, it works both as a course book and a work book that you can guide students through, individually or in groups. Since it contains so many exercises and activities, the students can be set on their way and left to work through each unit, consulting you as necessary. This will depend on the age of the students and the amount of musical experience they have already had on their instrument. Most teenagers and adults using this book will find that they should be able to work fairly independently.

Students of all ages should enjoy answering the short questions, doing the quizzes and puzzles and exercises along the way. This course is designed to allow students to perform lots of musical activities and check their answers by themselves. The answers to all activities are at the end of the book.

There are seven units in this course, each of which should be a month's work. At the end of each unit, the student should hand in their revision paper to the teacher for marking. That is all the marking you need do, although teachers will probably want to look over the student's work as they progress through each unit. This procedure transforms actual marking from weekly to monthly.

Given that many young music students are bright and have a broad interest in the world, they should find this book refreshing and stimulating. This course is bigger than most Musicianship courses. While it prepares students to pass the exam, it also aims to develop a concept of what music is. Those who remember the 'old maths' will know what this means. Nowadays maths is taught as a practical and useful part of life. This book aims to serve as a similar corrective to this in music theory.

Finally, this book is not written exclusively for AMEB Musicianship. Any student from about ten should be able to work through this book and enjoy doing so if they are at all interested in music. Many secondary schools like to ensure that the whole form has covered the rudiments of music. For example, it would be practical for all of year seven to work through this book without the burden of excessive marking for you. Many students starting elective music in years eight, nine or eleven will find the essentials that they need for those courses in this book.

The songs chosen for study mostly come from Alan Brandon's *Fifty Folk Songs* as these are the AMEB's test tunes. However there is also a wide range of other music throughout the book.

♪ To the Student   *Be a Muso!*

This course is for people who want to learn music so that they can become involved in it and its world. This means playing and singing and moving and listening and composing and improvising and reading and thinking and understanding and everything. It means doing. If you think you can learn music by reading some information and doing a test, then *put this book down now*. This book is for doers, for people who like to explore their world and discover things for themselves. Although this course book was written to fulfil the requirements of the AMEB syllabus, a syllabus is only a guide to the minimum expected and this course is broader than its syllabus.

Be prepared to enjoy yourself. Be active: clapping, stamping, singing, playing, shouting, talking to yourself, walking, running, recording yourself, pondering and working things out for yourself.

Introduction

This is what some great minds have to say on the matter of learning:

♪ Walter Gropius, a great German architect (1883–1969) said, 'The mind is like an umbrella—it functions best when open.' So, apart from being active, the other ingredient is an open mind.

♪ As the Old Oriental saying goes:

I hear and I forget;
I see and I remember;
I do and I understand.

As a student, you are not inventing music from the raw materials yourself. You are not re-inventing the wheel. You are entering a world that already exists with its organisation of sound, its goods and bads, rights and wrongs, its expectations of what a musician is, what he/she can do and what he/she knows. Musicians are worldly people who do not shun knowledge. Your ability to understand NEW things is greater the more things you already know. As they say, the more branches there are on a tree, the greater the possibility for new branches to grow. Enjoy your knowledge.

Some advice for students of anything: noticing things is one of the greatest aids to memory you can develop. If you don't know what colour socks you're wearing now, it's not another example of your bad memory (as many people would say), it's because you didn't pay much attention when you were putting them on. This book gives you the chance to notice things all the time and checks that you do. Read on.

We spend a lot of our lives needing to remember things. If you really take note of them in the first place, they have got at least as far as your short term memory. If you repeat the noticing, the information has got a greater chance of reaching your long term memory. This book will help you do that.

How to use this book

There are seven units and each one consists of lessons which you complete and mark yourself. Give yourself generous ticks and crosses. Put one in the margin *here* as a reminder. When you get to the end of a unit, do the revision paper and hand the book to your teacher for marking. Your teacher will also look through the unit to see if there are any problems that need clearing up.

Planning

You will probably need about four weeks to work through each unit. This makes it a seven month course. If you are preparing for an exam, count the exam date as month eight. Don't forget holidays and other things that happen during the year that might interrupt your study. You should be able to count back from the exam date and establish a realistic program for yourself.

You should also consult with your teacher (or the published syllabus) and note which folk songs you are required to be able to write out from memory. Write down the three folk songs required this year here:

_____, _____, and _____

If you are not using this book for the AMEB exam, you might like to agree with your teacher on some different songs.

Discovering Musicianship Grade One

Welcome to Unit One

In this unit we will

discover the notes on a keyboard
draw treble clefs on staves
learn the first nine notes
do a crossword
learn new words in two languages
name and draw notes
play a round

♪ Notes on a Keyboard

One of the most important things to understand from the beginning is note names.

1 Consider the keyboard. What do you already know? Complete as much as you can.

   a How many notes are there on a piano (white and black)? _____

   b Do notes exist that are higher and lower than those on the piano? _____

   c How many letter names are used in music? _____

   d What are they? _____

   e What happens when you get to the last of these? _____

   f What is the white note to the left of two black notes called? _____

   g What is the white note to the left of three black notes called? _____

   h By saying the musical alphabet, A to G, follow the white note names along the keyboard.

2 **a** Write the notes on the keyboard. Remember that the musical alphabet goes from A to G.

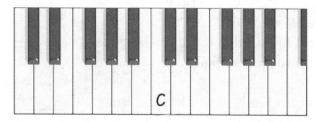

Now, on a separate piece of paper practise drawing keyboards yourself.

   b Think of some words you can spell just using the seven letters of the musical alphabet, such as E D G E.

   E D G E _____ _____ _____

   _____ _____ _____ _____

Discovering Musicianship Grade One

Unit One

♪ The Treble Clef, Lines and Spaces

Try to make your treble clefs as much like the printed ones as possible. Look at the example below.

3   a Which line does it wind around? _____
    b On which line does it cross itself? _____
    Your treble clefs should do the same. You will need quite a bit of practice at these. Now practise your treble clefs here:

The lines you have been practising your treble clefs on is called a **staff**. Look at the example above and answer these questions:

4   a How many lines make up a staff? _____
    b How many spaces are there between the lines? _____
    c Add these two numbers up to get _____
    d Each one of these positions can have a note on it. The lines from bottom to top are E G B D F. Can you work out the names of the notes that would go in the spaces? Use your alphabetical knowledge to fill in the gaps. What word do these four notes spell?
    ____ ____ ____ ____
    e There are nine notes, and only seven letter names. Which two are doubled up? _____ & _____

> ♪ A mnemonic is a phrase or rhyme that helps you remember something. Make up your own mnemonic for the lines—one word for each letter:
>
> E_____ G_____
>
> B_____ D_____
>
> F_____ .

5   a Using the information you've just learnt, write down the names of these notes. The first one has been done for you.

E

2   *Discovering Musicianship Grade One*

b Now try naming these notes by yourself:

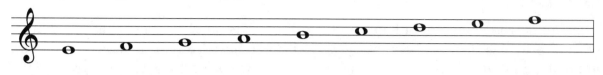

6 When you are learning to read music it is most important to recognise the notes quickly. These notes are out of alphabetical order, see how well you can remember their names:

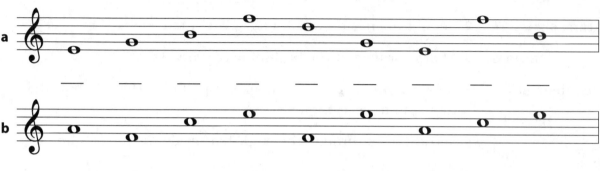

7 a Without looking up, write the note names on the line below the staff:

b Without looking, which notes are there two of? ____ & ____

8 Now name these notes.

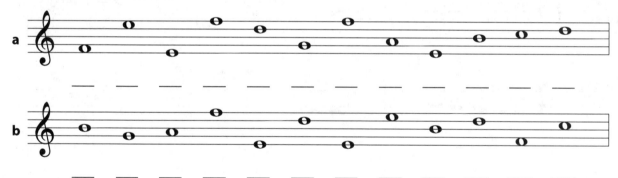

Treble Clefs

9 Draw a series of well-made treble clefs on this staff.

10 The treble clef has another name that is based on a letter from the musical alphabet. The other name comes from the name of the line the clef winds around. What letter do you think it is? ____

Discovering Musicianship Grade One

Unit One

♪ Vocabulary

Read this list of words and definitions carefully. If there is anything here that you don't know, don't hesitate to use a music dictionary (if you don't have your own music dictionary you should be able to find one in your local or school library). Draw lines matching the words with their correct definitions and check your answers. Don't worry if you don't know the words in the left column. Feel free to make mistakes, it's all part of learning.

11
- **a** key signature
- **b** time signature
- **c** barlines
- **d** double barline
- **e** bass clef
- **f** staff
- **g** treble clef
- **h** tempo

1. An Italian word that means 'speed'
2. Set of five lines on which music is written
3. Sharps or flats at the beginning of every line
4. A pair of numbers placed one on top of the other to show the timing in a piece of music
5. Vertical lines through the staff that divide the music into bars
6. 𝄞
7. Two vertical lines marking the end of a piece or a section of music
8. 𝄢

i Now use the above words to label the beginning of another Minuet by Bach.

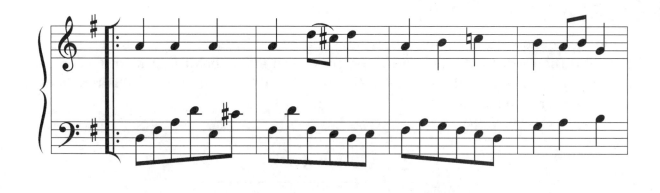

More Vocabulary

Staff notation is a collection of musicals symbols telling you *what* to play but they do not tell *how* to play. Italian words are used for this.

Here are some of the first words you need to know. The Italian words need to be matched with their English equivalents. Match what you can first. Then read the tips below and make your educated guesses.

12 a   lento   1 Gradually getting louder
    b   forte   2 At a moderate speed
    c   allegro   3 Loud
    d   crescendo   4 At an easy walking pace
    e   staccato   5 Slow
    f   andante   6 Quick, lively and fast
    g   piano   7 Soft
    h   moderato   8 Short and detached

Tips
- One word is almost the same in both languages: not *piano*.
- The Italian word for 'walk' is *andare* and for 'grow' is *crescere*.
- The piano's full name is *pianoforte* because it can play softly and loudly, something keyboard instruments before it couldn't do. The instrument Johann Sebastian Bach played was a harpsichord. No matter how hard you strike the keys on a harpsichord, the notes all sound at the same volume. In fact, Bach tried out an early piano and felt that it had little future. How wrong can you be!

Discovering Musicianship Grade One

Unit One

♪ Crossword—Reading Notes

13 Now for some more note reading fun, try this crossword by naming the notes on the staves below and then writing the answer in the crossword at the point indicated. For example, once you have named the three notes at **C6 across** go to **C6** in the crossword and write them in. **E7** has been done for you.

Across

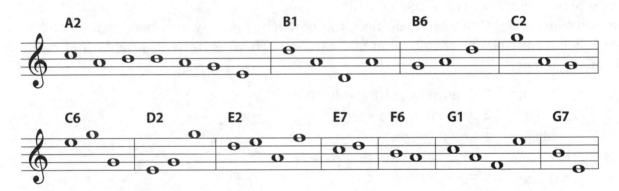

Down

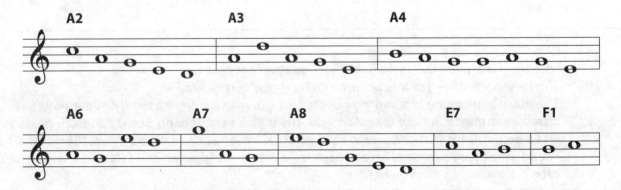

6 Discovering Musicianship Grade One

♪ Steady Note Naming

Steady Note Naming is an opportunity to name the notes at a regular speed. If you have a metronome, set it to a speed you can handle. Name the notes one per tick. Don't rush through it, but try to build your speed at note naming gradually. If you don't have a metronome, you can still work with the notes at an even speed that you control yourself.

A very handy little trick here is to do the last three notes (1) over and over until they are right and then the last six (2) over and over until they are right and then the last nine (3) and then the whole line. Use this procedure for every staff.

What is a Metronome?

A metronome is a timer that musicians use to establish the speed of the beat. As the metronome ticks away it gives a precise beat that is relative to one minute. It was invented in 1816 by J.N. Maelzel. You will often see the speed of music indicated by M.M. ♩ = 90. M.M. stands for Maelzel's Metronome.

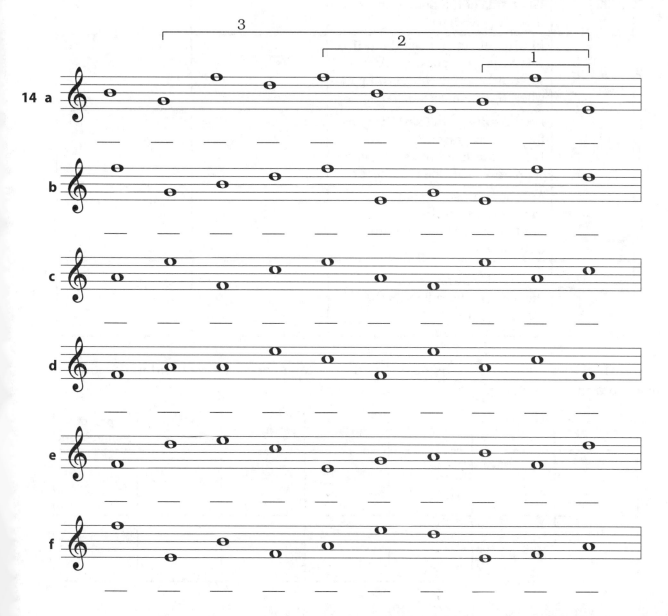

Discovering Musicianship Grade One

Unit One

♪ Drawing Notes

15 Have a good look at the notes in the first column, then read the questions in the second. Write your answer in the third column and draw the notes in the fourth.

		Question	Answer	Copy
a	𝑜	Is the semibreve a circle, a square, a triangle or an oval?		
b	𝅗𝅥 𝅗𝅥	Does the minim have the same **note head** shape as the semibreve? If not, how does it differ? Explain		
c	♩ ♩	What side of the crotchet is the **stem** when it goes up? What side of the note is the stem when it goes down?		
d	♪ ♪	In what direction does the **tail** go when the stem goes up? And in what direction does the **tail** go when the stem goes down?		
e	𝅘𝅥𝅯 𝅘𝅥𝅯	Do the **tails** go the same way as they do for quavers? Is the **note head** the same as the semibreve's OR the crotchet's?		
f	♫ ♫	Are the **beams** the same thickness as the **stems**? Are the upward **stems** on the right or left?		
g	𝅘𝅥𝅰𝅘𝅥𝅰 𝅘𝅥𝅰𝅘𝅥𝅰	Are the downward **stems** on the left? Are both **beams** the same thickness?		

Draw each of these notes again, using a ruler in the top space and freehand in the lower space: stems up and stems down.

semibreve	minim	crotchet	quaver	semiquaver	pair of quavers	pair of semiquavers

8   *Discovering Musicianship Grade One*

16 How is it that stems can go up OR down? Turn back to the Bach Minuet on page 4 and 5 and see if you can discover when the stems go up, and when they go down?

_____

_____

Tallis' Canon

17 Add stems to these noteheads. Remember to pay attention to left and right side as well as to the direction. A full copy of this song can be found in Unit Three under Scale Degree Numbers.

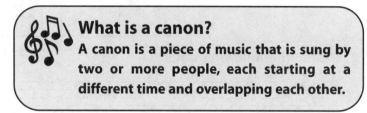

What is a canon?
A canon is a piece of music that is sung by two or more people, each starting at a different time and overlapping each other.

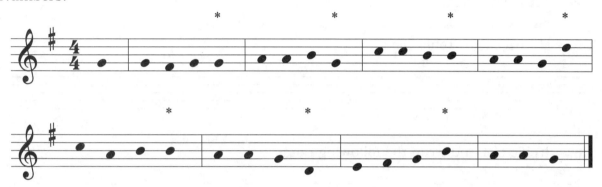

Try singing and playing this canon. You can do it with other musicians, starting one after the other at the asterisks (*).

Now turn to Revision Worksheet One. So far, you have been able to mark all the work that you have done yourself. Answers are not provided for the revision worksheets. On completion, hand it to your teacher.

Revision Worksheet One

1 Write the names of all the white notes on this keyboard.

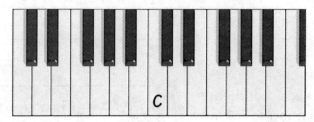

2 Name the following notes.

3 Draw eight excellent treble clefs.

4 Draw a treble clef and write the following notes.

E   D   G   A   C   F   E   D   B   F   G   A

5 Give definitions of the following words.

forte _____

treble clef _____

crescendo _____

barline _____

allegretto _____

tone _____

tempo _____

staccato _____

staff _____

6 Show your teacher how quickly you can name the notes on page 7.

Welcome to Unit Two

In this unit we will

learn notes beyond the staff
do a crossword
accent beats
meet rhythmic values
meet a dot
do some arithmetic
start working with time signatures
learn songs from around the world
learn some more Italian

♪ Leger Lines

So far, we have learned how many notes there are on the lines and in the spaces of a staff, but there are many more notes than this.

1 a Do you remember how many notes there are on a full piano keyboard? _____

To learn some more notes, we need to know about leger lines. These are the little lines, above or below the staff, that notes are drawn on. You are probably familiar with the famous Middle C. It is the note that piano lessons begin with.

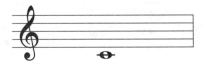

The famous Middle C

You already know the first three notes on this staff (below).

b Write their names on the line provided.

c Work through the musical alphabet to name the other notes. If you need further help, refer to the keyboard diagram in Unit One.

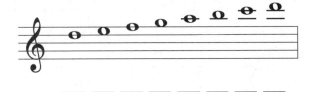

As you can see, the notes are going up. As you play the notes you'll hear them going up. But on a musical instrument, they don't feel like they are going up. On a keyboard, for example, going up means to the right and going down means to the left.

Discovering Musicianship Grade One   **11**

Unit Two

Of course, the same principle applies in the example where the notes are going down.

d Name the first three notes here. As soon as you name those first three notes, you will realise that we have to go backwards through the alphabet.

e Write all eight notes on the line provided.

You can now link all fifteen white notes in this two octave scale of C major to the keyboard. Draw a line from the keyboard to the matching note. One has been done for you.

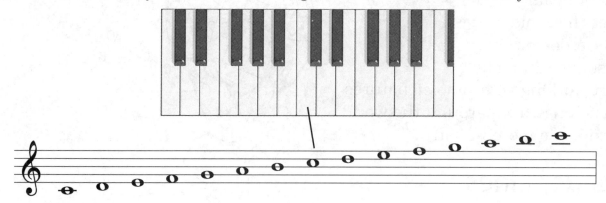

2 Name the notes on the following staves.

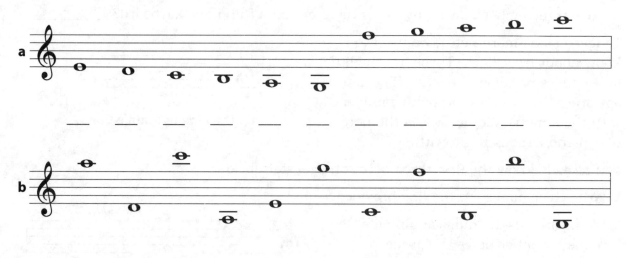

Steady Note Naming II

3 Now practise your steady note naming.

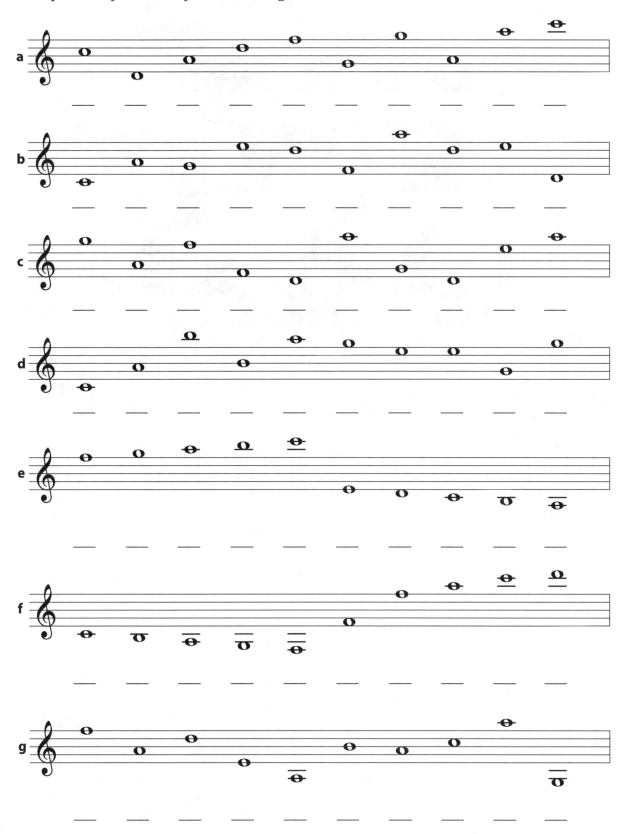

Unit Two

♪ Crossword—Leger Lines

Across

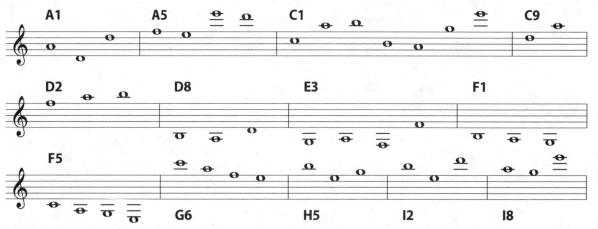

Down

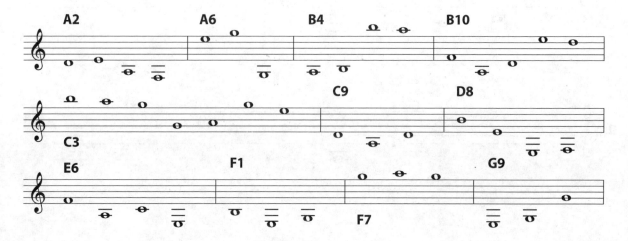

Discovering Musicianship Grade One

Note Value Names

5 We now need to look at duration or timing in music. The first step is to learn the names and values of the notes. You did this in Unit One. Try to remember the names and write them on the lines provided. See how many you can do by yourself.

Note name	a S _____	b M _____	c C _____	d Q _____
Picture of note	o	𝅗𝅥	♩	♪
Beats	e ___ crotchets	f ___ crotchets	g ___ crotchet	h half a crotchet

6 a Which notes have stems? _____
    b Which notes have tails? _____
    c Which notes are filled in? _____
    d Which ones aren't filled in? _____

7 Now have a look at this pyramid of values and you'll see how the notes relate. You can see that two semiquavers take the same space as one quaver and that four semiquavers take the same space as one crotchet. You can see that two crotchets take the same space as one minim and that eight quavers take the same space as one semibreve, and so on.

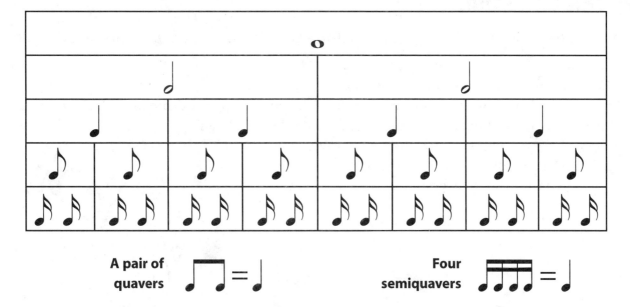

    a There are ____ quavers in a minim and ____ crotchets in a semibreve.
    b There are ____ crotchets in a minim and ____ quavers in a semibreve.
    c There are ____ quavers in a crotchet and ____ minims in a semibreve.

Unit Two

8 Let's do some arithmetic. Add up the values of each bar. For example, **a** is 1 + 2 + 1 = 4. Write your answers in the SUM column below and fill in the other columns.

Bar	First note in the bar	Last note in the bar	Sum of the values	Note name
a	crotchet		4 crotchets	
b			crotchets	
c		quaver	crotchets	C
d			crotchets	
e			crotchets	
f			crotchets	

Try This Little Quiz

9 A semi**circle** is half a _____, a semi**tone** is half a tone and a semi**quaver** is a half a _____.

Does that mean that a semibreve is half a _____?
Yes it does. And there's more. Breve comes from the Latin word *brevis* which means brief.
But if it's twice as long as a semibreve, how could it be brief?
Maybe there are longer notes than the breve.
As Fats Waller would say 'one never knows, do one?'
See page 92 for the answers!

♪ The Dot

A **dotted note** refers to one that has a dot written on the right of it. The dot indicates one special thing and it is to do with the length of the note. Let's discover what it is.

10 In this melody, there are four bars and each bar needs exactly FOUR crotchet beats.

Bar	1	2	3	4
Add up the values of each bar. How many beats are there in each bar?	3			
How much more is needed to add up to 4?	1	½		
Draw one note that would complete this bar.				

11 Do the same thing with this melody. Once again each bar should have four beats in it.

Bar	1	2	3	4
How many beats in each bar so far?	3½			
What is missing?				

Dots can supply those missing values

12 Add up the values of these notes once a dot has been added to them. The first one has been done for you.

  a semibreve   4   dotted semibreve: _4_ + _2_ = _6_
  b minim   2   dotted minim: ___ + ___ = ___
  c crotchet   1   dotted crotchet: ___ + ___ = ___

13 Can you explain the value of the dot? If not, don't worry, the answer is on page 93.

_____

_____

14 Now add the necessary dots to complete the two melodies above.

Unit Two

♪ Time Signatures

Read through the cartoon above and answer the following questions.

15 a Which beat in a bar is usually accented? First, last or something else? _____

   b How do we know which beat should be accented? _____

A **time signature** is placed at the beginning of a piece of music telling the player how many beats and what type of beats there are in each bar.
Copy the bars exactly as they are onto the staff beside them.

This time signature says that there can be two crotchets per bar or any grouping that adds up to two crotchets. This particular bar meets the basic requirements.

This time signature says that there can be three crotchets per bar, or any grouping that adds up to three crotchets.

This is the most common time signature and indicates that there can be four crotchets in a bar.

4/4 can also be written as C which stands for common time.

16 a What is placed at the beginning of the music to show the number and type of beats in a bar? _____

b Is it written at the beginning of **every** staff? _____

17 Add barlines to make each bar the right length according to the time signature in the two melodies by Mozart that follow. Notice that stems sometimes go up, sometimes down.

Variations on a Theme of Gluck K455 for pianoforte

a

Sonata in F for organ

b

18 Look at the following tunes which have barlines but no time signatures. Can you tell what the time signature should be for these? Write them after the key signature. These melodies don't have double barlines because they are just the beginning of long pieces.

Mozart—Menuett

a

Bach—Arioso

b

Sur Le Pont

19 In this copy of the famous French folk song *Sur le Pont*, there are no barlines. You will need to add them. The time signature tells you that after every two beats there must be a barline. Don't forget the *special* barline at the end of the piece.

Discovering Musicianship Grade One

Kookaburra

20 The barlines are missing from this well-known Australian song. Add them according to the time signature. *Kookaburra* is actually a canon. Can you remember the canon that was introduced in Unit One? Try playing and singing *Kookaburra* as a canon.

21 What purpose does a time signature serve?

_____

_____

_____

Unto Us Is Born A Son

22 In this carol, you see everything except the barlines, the time signature and the words.

Sing or play it through and put an accent sign (>) under or over each of the accented beats—all the ones that you feel are a bit stronger than others. The first three are done for you. They should fall into a regular pattern.

You should be able to put in the barlines now. How many beats do you find in each bar? Add your time signature. See page 94 for a clue if you get stuck.

You'll have to experiment a bit to work this out. Trying is an important part of learning.

Shepherds Awaken

23 Play this carol or clap the rhythm. Work out the time signature, and add the barlines.

Terminology

24 Italian words are used internationally in music. They give musicians different instructions on how to perform a piece of music. Some of them tell us what speed to play at (tempo), others about changing the speed, others about the volume of the music and others about how to play particular notes.

Tempo (speed)	Speed Changing	Dynamics (volume)	Other

Look at the words now and copy them into the columns where they belong (above). There are two words for each direction.

legato smoothly; *mezzo piano* moderately soft; *moderato* at a moderate speed; *rallentando* gradually getting slower; *staccato* play the notes short, do not connect them smoothly; *diminuendo* gradually getting softer; *ritardando* slower; *allegro* quick, lively and bright.

Now that you have finished Unit Two, complete the Revision Worksheet for this unit.

♪ Revision Worksheet Two

1 **a** Write the names of all the white notes on the keyboard below.
    b Write the names of all the notes on the staff.
    c Using a ruler, join the notes from the staff to the notes on the keyboard.

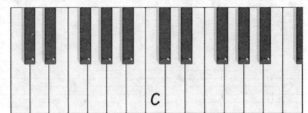

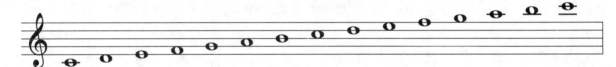

2 What type of notes are in the scale (above)? Semibreves, minims, crotchets, quavers?

_____

3 Name these notes.

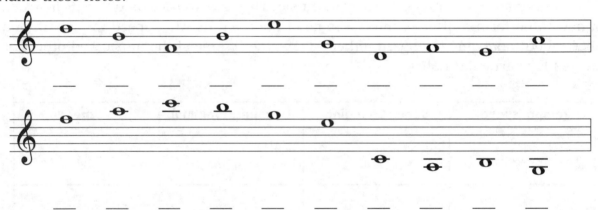

4 Using the notes written below the staff, complete the following activity.
    a Draw a treble clef at the beginning of the staff.
    b All notes are minims. Write the first five **above** the staff and the next five **below** using leger lines.

        C   A   B   D   G   G   C   D   A   B

5 Which type of note has:
    a A filled-in note head with a stem but no tail _____
    b A stem and a hollow note head _____
    c A hollow note head only _____
    d A filled-in note head and a stem and a tail _____
    e A filled-in note head with a stem and two tails _____

22   *Discovering Musicianship Grade One*

Revision Worksheet Two

    f When the stem goes down is it on the left or right?

    g When the stem goes up is it on the left or right?

    h Which direction does the tail go in when the stem goes down?

    i Which direction does the tail go in when the stem goes up?

    j Which type of note is spelled the same forwards and backwards?

6 Fill in the following table. Write your answer in the third column.

	How many ...	are there in a ...	Total
a	quavers	crotchet	
b	quavers	dotted minim	
c	crotchets	dotted minim	
d	minims	dotted semibreve	
e	quavers	dotted crotchet	
f	crotchets	semibreve	

7 What effect does a dot have when placed beside a note?

8 Beside each bar, write one note that has the same value as it.

Revision Worksheet Two

9 a Does a time signature indicate tempo? _____

  b Is 4/4 faster **or** slower than 2/4 **or** neither? _____

  Explain: _____

10 Give a time signature to each of these four rhythm patterns.

11 Put barlines in the following rhythms.

Revision Worksheet Two

12 All of the bars in these rhythms are incomplete. Complete each one by adding a dot to one note only.

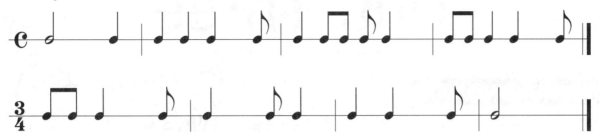

13 Complete the following table.

Note name	semibreve (whole note)	minim (half note)	_____ (quarter note)	quaver (_____ note)
Value				
Note				

The words in parentheses are used by Americans and continental Europeans (in their own languages).

14 Draw a pair of quavers in the oblong. In the square, draw the note that has the same value as the pair of quavers.

15 Which bars in *Frère Jacques* have only got quavers in them? _____

16 Write the time signatures of these songs in the space provided. Do this from memory.

Sur le Pont _____   Shepherds Awaken _____

Unto us is born a Son _____   Tallis' Canon _____

Kookaburra _____

Ask your teacher to tell you which song you will need to be able to write out from memory by the time you get to Revision Worksheet Three. These change every year for examinations.

Discovering Musicianship Grade One

Welcome to Unit Three

In this Unit we will

work with **black** notes:
  on the keyboard
  on the staff
    drawing them
    naming them
    writing them
    using them
meet keys and scales,
  accidentals and
  scale degree numbers
meet intervals and
  tones and semitones
features of musical notation

♪ Black Notes

Yes, I prefer the black ones too.

Turn this box into a two octave keyboard, starting on C. Draw the vertical lines first, leaving 1cm per white note, then add the black notes. Write the numbers 1 to 10 across the top of the keyboard above the **black notes**. Refer to earlier diagrams if you need to.

Enter Sharps, Flats and Naturals

Read through the following sentences and circle the correct answers.

1 a ♯ A sharp is one step <u>higher or lower</u> than a note with the same letter name. Is the sound <u>higher or lower</u> and is the direction on the keyboard to the <u>left or right</u>?

b ♭ A flat is one step <u>higher or lower</u> than a note with the same letter name. The sound is <u>higher or lower</u> and the direction on the keyboard is to the <u>left or right</u>.

c ♮ The third symbol is a natural sign and it cancels a sharp or flat. It means 'play a white note' in piano terms.

Fill in the spaces with very neat copies of the sharp, flat and natural.

♯						
♭						
♮						

d Complete this table of notes by referring to the numbers you wrote above the keyboard on page 26.

Black note number	Sharp name	Flat name
1 and 6		
2 and 7	D♯	
3 and 8		
4 and 9		A♭
5 and 10		

Practise drawing these notes on the staff below, making sure that they only cross the line or space that they are meant to be on or in.

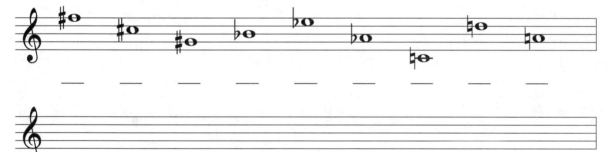

Note: when you write sharps, flats and naturals on the staff, they go on the _____ side of the note. But when you write them with letter names, they go on the _____, for example, F♯.

e Now write the names of the notes underneath the staff.

Discovering Musicianship Grade One

Unit Three

♪ Using Sharps, Flats and Naturals

Have a look at the melodies in this book and you will notice that many of them have sharps or flats after the clef on each stave. The sharps or flats in this position are the **key signature**. We are about to see how this tells us what sharps or flat to play.

I Had a Little Nut Tree

2   a How many sharps are in the key signature of the melody below? _____

    b What two sharps does the key signature have? _____ and _____

    c Name the last note of the piece: _____

    d Circle all the notes that would be played as sharps.

A Farmer's Son

3   This piece has one flat.

    a What flat is it? _____

    b What is the last note? _____

    c Circle the three notes that would be played as flats.

4   Join all the notes that have the same sound, or the same keyboard note. One is done for you.

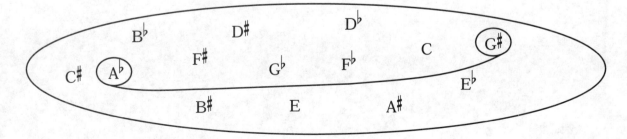

28   *Discovering Musicianship Grade One*

5 When sharps, flats or naturals are written during a piece of music they are referred to as **accidentals**. How long does an accidental last?

  a Only for the note it is attached to?
  b For the rest of the piece or section?
  c For the rest of the bar it is in?

For example, if you use a sharp to make a G into a G♯, any other Gs after it will sound as G♯ until the barline. But only that G, not Gs in other octaves. Gs in other octaves will not be sharpened unless they have their own ♯. The same applies to flats and naturals.

6 a Look at this little Allegro, and circle all the notes that are played as G♯ and put a square around all the notes that are played as G. If you can play it, do so.

  b Which side of notes are accidentals written on? _____
  c Which side of letter names? _____

♪ Scale Degree Numbers

7 In **C major**, C is 1, D is 2, E is 3, ___ is 4, ___ is 5, ___ is 6, ___ is 7, ___ is 8. Write the numbers under this scale.

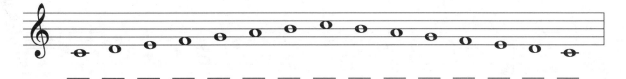

8 a Is the number for F the same when the scale is ascending as when it is descending? _____
  b Turn back to Activities 10 and 11 on page 17 where there are two short melodies in C major. Write the scale degree numbers under them.

Unit Three

9 a In **G major**, G is 1, A is 2, ___ is 3, ___ is 4, ___ is 5, ___ is 6, ___ is 7, ___ is 8.
Write the numbers under this scale.

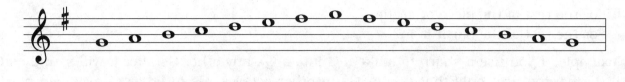

b Is the number for D the same when the scale is ascending as when it is descending? ____

c Is B the same number ascending and descending? ____

10 Turn back to Tallis' Canon on page 9 and write the scale degree numbers under each note. The last bar ends in 2 2 1.

11 a In **F major**, F is 1, G is 2, ___ is 3, ___ is 4, ___ is 5, ___ is 6, ___ is 7, ___ is 8.

b Write the numbers under this scale.

c Are the numbers for D and A the same when the scale is ascending as when it is descending? _____

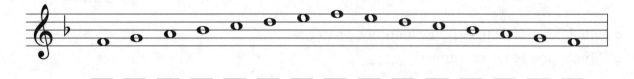

This Old Man

12 Write the scale degree numbers under this tune.

30   *Discovering Musicianship Grade One*

♪ Intervals

13 The distance from one note to another is called an **interval**. These are mostly named according to ordinal numbers, that is, first, second, third, and so on. The first, however, is called **unison** and the last is called **octave**.

The lower note in an interval is always 1. The next note along is second, then third and so on. Look at these scales and count the interval between them in the space provided.

a From E to F is a _____

d From B to G is a _____

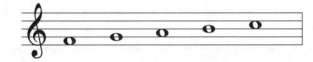

b From F to C is a _____

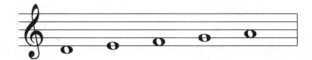

e From D to A is a _____

c From A to F is a _____

♪ Two Types of Seconds—Tones and Semitones

14 Think about what we said 'semi-' meant when we were discussing quavers and semiquavers on page 16.

  a What must the difference be between a tone and semitone: 1 tone = ___ semitones. Look at a keyboard and compare G to A and B to C. As A is one note away from G, and C is one note away from B, they are both seconds.

  b There is a difference, however—can you see what it is?

  _____

  When there is one note in between (black or white), the interval is called a **tone**. If there is no note in between, as with B to C, then it is called a **semitone**.

  c So, the two types of seconds are _____ and _____.

  d What is the smallest interval? _____

  e Draw a box around the notes here that **do not** have another note between them. Circle the pair that is neither a tone nor a semitone.

    E F♯   G♯ A   B C   F G♯   B♭ C   D♭ E♭

Unit Three

♪ Let's Discover Keys and Scales

As we've already seen, most pieces have either sharps or flats between the clef and the time signature. Pieces usually end on a specific note which is related to those sharps or flats. Complete this table, looking over some of the music in units one to three. Find pieces that have key signatures of one sharp, two sharps etc, and write their names into the middle column. On the right, name the last note of the pieces. Two have been done as examples.

Key signature	Songs or pieces you know (at least two)	Last note of the piece
no ♯ or ♭		
1 ♯	Hot Cross Buns	G
2 ♯s	I had a little nut tree	D
3 ♯s		
1 ♭		

- The last note in these cases is the key note of the piece. Another word for the key note is **tonic**.
- The last note is not always the tonic, although this is very rare.

If you take all the notes used in a piece of music and list them in alphabetical order, you'll end up with a **scale**. Nearly all music that has pitch (melody and harmony) is based on scales. The two types of scales that western classical music is based on are **major** and **minor** scales.

Good King Wenceslas

15 Write the note names under all of the notes of *Good King Wenceslas*. Ignore the numbers here, they will be used in the next section.

32   *Discovering Musicianship Grade One*

Now work through the following steps using *Good King Wenceslas*.

Step One: List in alphabetical order all the notes in the song, using the last note of the song as your first letter.

___ ___ ___ ___ ___ ___ ___ ___ ___

Step Two: Circle the pairs of notes (letters) that are a *semitone* apart. Remember, there are only ever two pairs of semitones in a major scale. They are between the 3rd and 4th notes and the 7th and 8th notes.

> There are only ever two pairs of semitones in a major scale.

Step Three: The notes that are a semitone apart are 3 & 4, 7 & 8. From this you can work out what 1 is. Is 1 the last note in the piece? Is it the tonic?

Result: You now know the key of the piece and can write its scale from the lower tonic to the upper tonic on this staff. Draw a treble clef and the key signature.

---

16 You need to go through the procedure again so it can be tested. Turn back to *I had a little nut tree* on page 28.

Step One: List all of the notes used in alphabetical order.

___ ___ ___ ___ ___ ___ ___ ___ ___

Step Two: Circle the pairs of notes (letters) that are a *semitone* apart.

Step Three: You know 3 & 4, 7 & 8. Work out from this what 1 is. If that's all fallen into place, you should find that 1 equals the last note of the piece.

Does 1 equal the last note? ____

Result: You now know the key of the piece and can write its scale from the lower tonic to the upper. Draw a treble clef and the key signature first.

♪ Revision

17 Before we discover anything new, complete these revision activities.
   a Practise drawing the musical symbols you have learned so far on the staff below. Draw one of each of the following symbols: treble clef, semibreve, minim, crotchet, quaver, semiquaver, a dotted crotchet, and a $\frac{2}{4}$ time signature.

Unit Three

b Between which pairs of scale degree numbers do the semitones in a major scale occur?
___ & ___ and ___ & ___

c When a piece of music has no sharps or flats in its key signature, what major key is it in? _____

d When a piece of music has one flat in its key signature, what major key is it in? _____

e Is it possible to have a major scale with semitones other than 3 & 4, 7 & 8? _____

f Scales are usually written in semibreves, one octave ascending, unless you are asked for something else. Also the semitones are indicated by **slurs**. These are curved lines linking the two notes of the semitone. You can see them in the first example below. Your task now is to copy the four scales very neatly and put the other slurs in place.

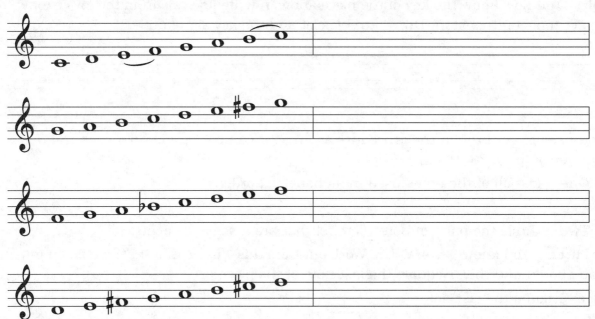

g You have just written four scales using accidentals. You should now write these scales again, but this time with key signatures. Include the slurs that show where the semitones occur.

34 *Discovering Musicianship Grade One*

Vocabulary

18 Match the definitions with the terms. You have not met all of these terms yet, so make educated guesses wherever you need to. Then label them on the stave wherever possible. These four bars come from the first of Fifteen Waltzes for Piano by Beethoven.

a	barlines	1	Suddenly
b	repeat sign	2	A sign placed at the beginning of a stave indicating that the second line of the staff is G
c	pause	3	A line joining notes of the same pitch telling the performer to hold for the duration of both notes
d	subito	4	A sign placed at the beginning of a stave indicating that the fourth line of the staff is F
e	treble clef	5	A sign which means that the note or rest must be held longer than usual
f	brace	6	Double barline with double dots indicating that the music is to be played again
g	bass clef	7	Sharps or flats at the beginning of every stave indicating the key of the piece
h	tie	8	Italian term for loud
i	forte	9	Set of five lines on which music is written
j	crescendo	10	Vertical lines dividing the music into bars
k	time signature	11	A pair of numbers at the beginning of a piece or section of music to indicate timing
l	key signature	12	A sign used to join a group of staves
m	staff	13	A sign indicating silence
n	rest	14	Italian term indicating getting louder

Discovering Musicianship Grade One

Revision Worksheet Three

1 Put barlines in the following rhythms.

2 Circle all the crotchet beats in these melodies. Then add the time signatures. Beware: one of the answers is a time signature that we have not so far encountered in this course.

3 Name the following intervals.

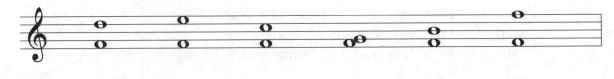

4 Write the first five intervals above C and the next five above G.

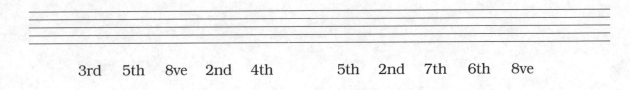

3rd 5th 8ve 2nd 4th   5th 2nd 7th 6th 8ve

5 None of these bars add up to the time signature. Complete them by adding one note at the end of each bar.

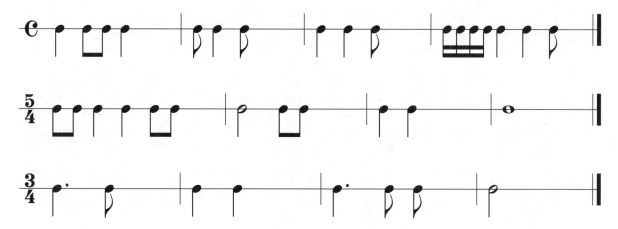

6 None of these bars adds up to the time signature. Dot one note in each bar to complete it.

7 Complete this table by drawing the note and writing its name in the first two columns.

Note	Name	Value
		4
		2
		1
		½
		¼

8 Write the scales of D major and F major, one octave descending on the staves below. Mark the semitones with slurs. Use key signatures.

Revision Worksheet Three

9 Write out one of the songs that you are supposed to know from memory on the staves below:

10 Circle all the notes in the melody that are played as F and put a square around all the notes that are played as F♯.

11 Give definitions of the following words:

rest _____

accelerando _____

crescendo _____

interval _____

octave _____

semitone _____

tonic _____

natural _____

Welcome to Unit Four

In this unit we will

meet the bass clef:
 on the keyboard
 on the stave
 on leger lines
do some crosswords
meet rests
revise intervals

♪ Enter the Bass Clef

1 a Do you remember how many notes there are on a piano? _____

  b How many notes can there be on a staff? four lines, five spaces, = _____. Plus a note above the staff and a note below is another _____ making a total of _____

  c We can put sharps and flats in front of all of these, making another _____. Clearly, it is the lower pitches that our treble clef notes are not dealing with.

Firstly, let's draw our own bass clefs. Use this staff to practise copying and drawing bass clefs. Try to make them as much like the printed ones as possible. Look at it closely. Which line does it wind around? Your bass clefs should do the same. You will need a bit of practice at these. You should use manuscript paper to practise further.

2 a Each one of the five lines and four spaces takes its own note. The lines from bottom to top are G B D F A. Would you like to make up your own mnemonic for this?

_____ _____ _____ _____ _____

Name the five notes that have been underlined:

Discovering Musicianship Grade One   39

Unit Four

b You can now work out the other notes yourself: ____ ____ ____ ____

Devise your own mnemonic for this one too.

_____ _____ _____ _____

The **bass clef** is used when the majority of notes are below middle C. Draw lines connecting the notes on the keyboard to the notes on the staff. One has been done for you as an example.

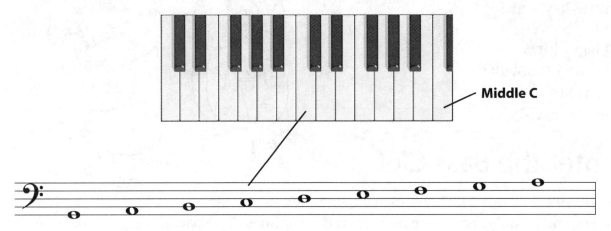

3 a Name the notes on the staff below.

____ ____ ____ ____ ____ ____ ____ ____

b Stem Direction: Observe the stem directions in the note naming exercise you have just done, then circle the correct word in the following sentence.

Do the notes above the middle line have their stems <u>up</u> or <u>down</u>? What about the notes below the middle line? _____

c Write the notes on the staff below using only the lines and spaces. No leger lines. Make all notes minims. The arrows indicate whether to write high or low A or G.

40   *Discovering Musicianship Grade One*

Steady Note Naming III

4 Name these notes.

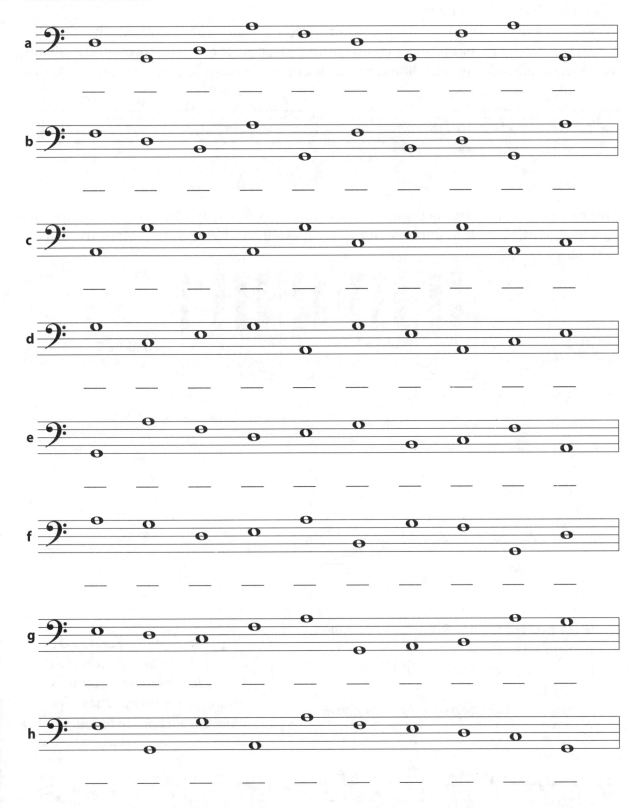

Unit Four

♪ Bass Clef Leger Lines

You know the principles of leger lines from your treble clef studies on page 11. Circle the correct answer in the following statements.

5 **a** When notes are descending, do you count <u>forwards/backwards</u> through the alphabet?
  b When the notes are ascending, do you count <u>forwards/backwards</u> through the alphabet?
  c Write the names of the leger line notes that appear here:

G _ _ _ _ _ G A _ _ _

  d You can now write a two octave scale of C major in the bass clef that will exactly match this keyboard. Write it in minims and space it evenly across the staff. Mark the semitones with slurs.

  e Name these notes without looking back.

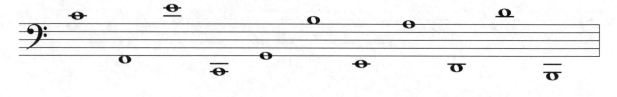

6 Here is an excerpt from a Suite for solo cello by Johann Sebastian Bach.
  a Write the note names under all the notes.
  b What key is it in? _____
  c Now write the scale degree numbers above the notes.

> The triple stopped notes occur when three notes are played at once on a string instrument. They are named from bottom to top.

42 *Discovering Musicianship Grade One*

♪ Crossword—Bass Clef Leger Lines

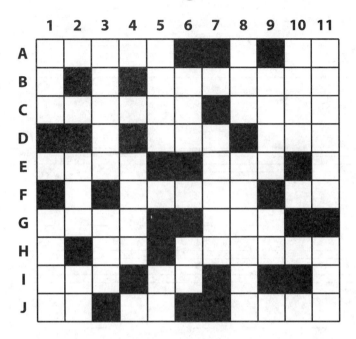

Across

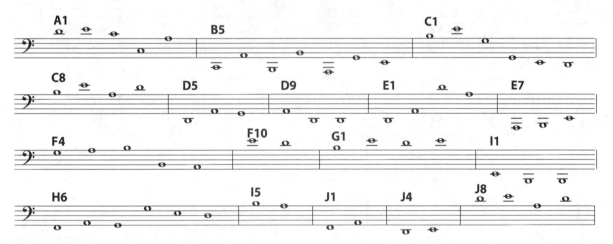

Down

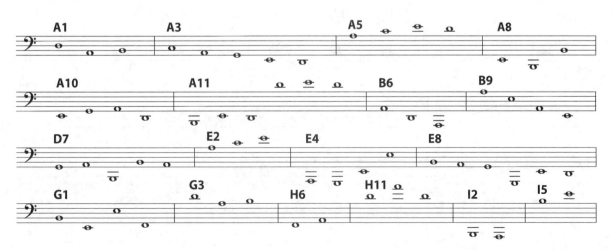

Unit Four

♪ Steady Note Naming IV

8 Name these notes.

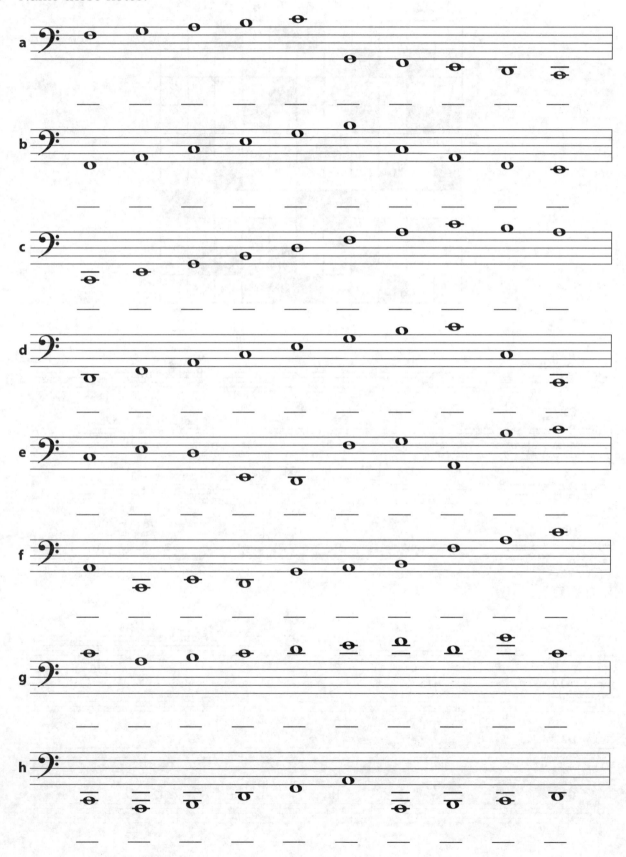

Discovering Musicianship Grade One

♪ Drawing Rests

9 Even though we haven't studied using rests yet, we shall use this notation lesson as an opportunity to find out a little about them. **Rests** are used to indicate silence in music and they have set lengths just as notes do. In the following table you need to state the number of beats, answer the question and copy the rests.

	Name	Beats	Rest	Question	Answers	Rest
a	Semibreve		▬ (on line)	What shape is this rest? Does it sit on or hang from a line? Which line?		
b	Minim		▬ (on line)	What shape is this rest? Does it sit on or hang from a line? Which line?		
c	Crotchet		𝄽	Do you start drawing it from the top or bottom? *Note*: When drawing this note freehand, you don't usually bother with the thick parts.		
d	Quaver		𝄾	Do you start drawing it from the top or bottom? Is the vertical line truly vertical?		
e	Semiquaver		𝄿	Do you add the second hook after you have drawn the quaver rest?		

f One of the rests in the table is also used for a complete bar of silence no matter what the time signature. Which one do you think it is? _____

Discovering Musicianship Grade One

Unit Four

♪ Rests in Music

> 'The notes I handle no better than many pianists. But the pauses between the notes—ah—that is where the art resides.'
>
> Arthur Schnabel (1958)
> A great twentieth-century pianist.

Silence is a very important musical resource. Used wisely, it can create all sorts of effects. There is a famous string quartet by Joseph Haydn called the Joke Quartet because he included lots of moments of silence towards the end of the piece. This was to trick the audience into applauding as soon as they 'heard' silence. He was tired of the lack of attention they paid while listening to his music. Another great use of silence is in the film music to *Jaws*. Those pauses between the short phrases create a devilish amount of tension.

10 Add up the values of each rhythm pattern below then match the pairs that have the same number of beats. Write the answers in the box below.

a	b	c	d	e

11 Complete these melodies with one rest at the end of each bar.

c Name the keys and describe the time signatures of these two staves (above). Now note all of the performance instructions by circling and labeling them. Use words such as: slow, major, pause, staccato, slur, tie etc.

♪ Intervals Revisited

12 a Complete the numbering of the scale here. See page 29 if you need help.

1 2 __ __ __ __ __ __ __ __ __ __ __ __ 2 1

The distance in pitch between any two notes, whether played at the same time or one after the other, has a name, in fact a number. The interval from the bottom note to any note in its scale is the same number as the scale degree but remember that ordinal numbers are used.

> Some people feel the urge to subtract the higher note from the lower note making G to B a 2nd instead of a 3rd. Don't be misled. Always count the bottom note as one and remember that zero is not used.

b Name these intervals.

G to B _____   G to D _____   G to F♯ _____

G to A _____   G to C _____   G to E _____

c Here is the scale of F major. Write the scale degree numbers under it.

d Name these intervals.

F to B♭ _____   F to D _____   F to G _____

F to A _____   F to C _____   F to E _____

e Name the note that is...

a 4th above D _____   a 5th above D _____   an 8ve above D _____

a 6th above D _____   a 7th above D _____   a 3rd above D _____

f Write the names of the intervals on the lines below the staff.

g Write notes above those provided in the following staff to form the intervals that have been named.

3rd   5th   2nd   7th   6th   4th   8ve   6th   3rd   7th

Discovering Musicianship Grade One

Unit Four

Frère Jacques

In *Frère Jacques* the barlines are missing. Put them in. Don't forget the double barline at the end. Then answer these questions about the song.

13 a What is the key signature? _____

    b What is the last note? _____

    c What key is this piece in? _____

    d What is the tonic in this piece? _____

    e What is the time signature? _____

    f Circle all the semitones in the odd numbered bars and box all the tones in the even bars. Write the scale degree numbers under all the notes.

    g Balance the seesaw by drawing the matching rest on the up side.

♪ Revision Worksheet Four

1. Put barlines in the following rhythms.

2. **a** Insert the time signatures into these excerpts.

   Et in spiritum from Mass in C minor by Mozart

   Tardi s'avende—La Clemenza di Tito by Mozart

   Gute Nacht from Jesu Meine Freude by Bach

   Chorale from Jesu Meine Freude by Bach

   b Can you state the keys of these pieces? The first two are major and the second two are minor. As they are excerpts only, do not expect them to finish on the tonic.

   _____ major, _____ major, _____ minor, _____ minor

   c Can you comment on the rest in bar 5 of the first piece?

   _____

Discovering Musicianship Grade One

Revision Worksheet Four

3 Write these notes in the treble clef on the upper staff and in the bass clef on the lower staff.

C   E   G   D   C   A   F   G   B   A   F   E   B

4 Write these intervals above G in the bass clef. Use accidentals where necessary.

8ve   5th   4th   7th   2nd   3rd   unison

5 Describe these signs fully.

p _____

f _____

♮ _____

𝄴 _____

𝄽 _____

6 Work out the time signature and add the barlines to this tune. Then name the tune and write the scale degree numbers underneath.

Welcome to Unit Five

In this unit we will

learn to divide words into syllables
do a lot of rhythm exercises
find the accented syllables in words and phrases
meet the anacrusis in verse and in rhythms
revise the bass clef
discover the art of transposition
work with some new vocabulary—and old

♪ Syllables in Words

1 Say the following twenty words out loud, counting the number of syllables in each word. Write the number of syllables beside it. The last one is done for you.

> A syllable is a unit of **sound**, either a word or a part of a word. The following words have been separated into their syllables: **Sing** has one syllable, **strict**ly has two and **um**brella has three, **auto**mobile has four, **incon**siderate has five.

	roamed		enviable		wonderful		style		crotchet
	thankfully		minim		stream		zany		tiger
	trumpet		barrister		wicked		Iowa		it
	keyboard		trundle		comedy		daffodil	3	overcoat

2 a Rewrite the words into the table below with hyphens separating the syllables. For example thankfully would look like this: thank-ful-ly.

one syllable	♪	
two syllables	♫	wick-ed
three syllables	♫♪	won-der-ful
four syllables	♫♫	

b When a word has more than one syllable, one of them is usually pronounced with a bit more stress (that is, a bit louder). Say these words again and underline the accented syllable.

Discovering Musicianship Grade One

Unit Five

The words you have just been looking at were especially chosen because of their **stress pattern**.

c Have another look at the twenty words and answer the following question.

True/False: The first syllable of **every** word in the list is stressed? _____

3 a Say the following words aloud and write the number of syllables on the left. Then underline the stressed syllables. The stresses in this activity occur on different parts of each word.

	reduce		musicianship		difficult		parrot
	circumstances		allegro		rallentando		transposition
	mountain		elephant		photographer		unfinished
	tambourine		national		cockatoo		parade

b Copy the words into the correct space. Don't forget to hyphenate each word.

Two syllables	Accented first	
	Accented second	
Three syllables	Accented first	
	Accented second	
	Accented third	
Four syllables	Accented first	
	Accented second	
	Accented third	

52   *Discovering Musicianship Grade One*

♪ Test Your Rhythm Memory

4 a Here are the rhythm and words of every second bar of *Frere Jacques*. When you sing the whole song through, you will recognise the missing bars. Your task is to complete the rhythm and words of this song. It's easier than you think!

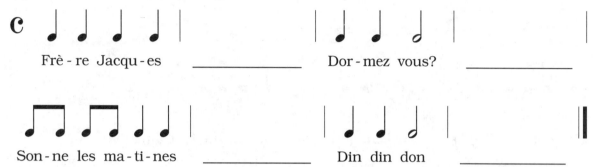

b Although *Sur le Pont* is eight bars long, it contains only two different bars of rhythm. They are given. Write the rest of the rhythm in and add the words exactly under the notes.

(lyrics)

If you are not familiar with the following songs, move onto the next activity.

Rhythm Exercises

5 a These bars have been labeled A–F. They belong to *This Old Man* and *Hot Cross Buns*. Some of the bars can be used in both songs. Clap or sing through the rhythms and the songs and work out the order of the bars.

Using the letters, write the order of the bars here:

This Old Man

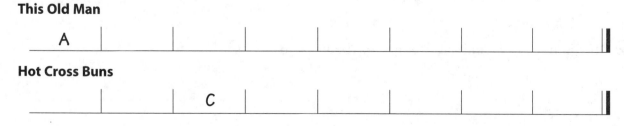

Hot Cross Buns

b This song is *Goe from My Window Goe*. Group the notes that belong to each beat then write the beat numbers as shown in the first two bars.

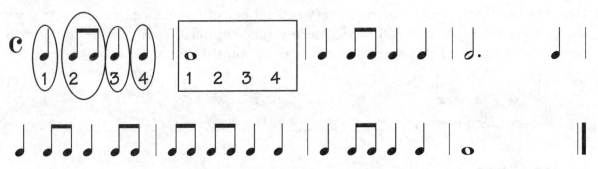

c This song is *Shepherds Awaken*, group the beats in the following piece.

♪ Accented Syllables in Verse

As we learnt in the first word activity, stresses can occur on different syllables. This also happens in *groups* of words. Sometimes the first word in a sentence or phrase is accented, sometimes it is not. Say the following lines out loud and place a vertical line in front of the first **strong** syllable you hear. The first one is done for you.

6   **a** In | sum - mer time when leaves grow green

     b Un - to us is born a Son

     c I had a lit - tle nut tree

     d A far - mer's son so sweet

     e Lav - en - der's blue dil - ly dil - ly

     f The holl - y and the iv - y

     g My name is Bob the swag - man

     h One night when trav - 'ling sheep

     i Then blow ye winds heigh ho!

     j My bon - nie lies over the o - cean

     k Oh She - nan - doah I long to hear you

Matching Up

7 Five of the phrases on the previous page go with the following melody beginnings. Match them, then check your answers. Then write the hyphenated words under the notes. Don't forget to answer the questions on the right.

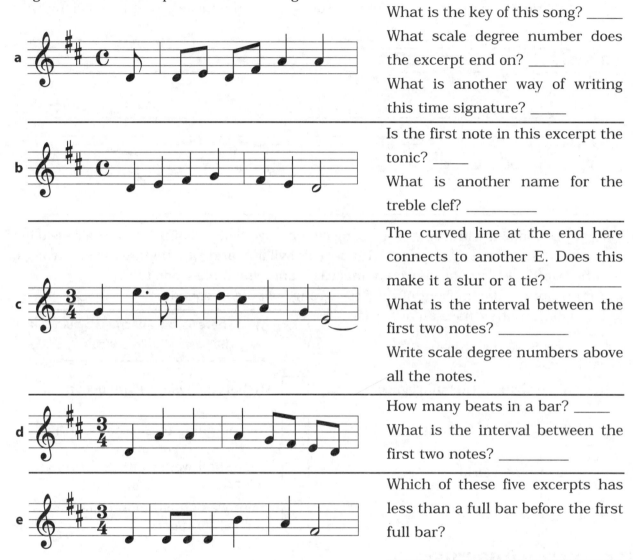

a) What is the key of this song? _____
What scale degree number does the excerpt end on? _____
What is another way of writing this time signature? _____

b) Is the first note in this excerpt the tonic? _____
What is another name for the treble clef? _____

c) The curved line at the end here connects to another E. Does this make it a slur or a tie? _____
What is the interval between the first two notes? _____
Write scale degree numbers above all the notes.

d) How many beats in a bar? _____
What is the interval between the first two notes? _____

e) Which of these five excerpts has less than a full bar before the first full bar?
_____

♪ The Anacrusis in Words and Phrases

Compare the openings of the two versions of *Waltzing Matilda*. Put a vertical (upright) line in front of the first strong syllable in each one.

Oh there once was a swagman camped by a billabong
vs
Once a jolly swagman camped by a billabong

The first version has an **anacrusis** but the second doesn't. What do you think the word anacrusis means? The word anacrusis refers to the note or notes before the first full bar. This usually happens in a song when the first accented syllable in a line is not the first syllable. We have already seen this occurring in words such as pho-to-graph-er and re-duce.

Discovering Musicianship Grade One

Unit Five

8 Have another look at the songs in Activity Seven. Name the three songs that have an anacrusis. _____

9 Look at the two melodies below. They are the first phrases of the two versions of *Waltzing Matilda*. One has an anacrusis and one doesn't, just as we noted with the words. Your task now is to write the correct version of the words under the melody that they belong with.

10 You may be familiar with some of the songs mentioned below. Think about their melody and try to work out which songs start with a weak syllable and which start with a strong one. In other words, which ones have an anacrusis and which ones don't?

  a Put an upright line in front of the first strong syllable in each one.
  b Tick (✔) those that have an anacrusis.

> There is an anacrusis when the first syllable is weak.

☐ God Save the Queen

☐ Australians let us all rejoice   ☐ My bonnie lies over the ocean

☐ O come all ye faithful   ☐ Are you going to Scarborough Fair

☐ Joy to the World   ☐ What shall we do with a drunken sailor?

☐ On Top of Old Smoky   ☐ There was an old man called Michael Finnigan

More on the Anacrusis

11 Here are the opening melodies for some of the songs just mentioned. Follow the instructions below:
  • Identify each song.
  • Write the words under the notes.
  • Discover where the strong beats occur by tapping the beat while you hum the tune.
  • Add the time signature and barlines. You will know whether there is an anacrusis from the accents in the verse.

Discovering Musicianship Grade One

♪ Bass Clef Revision

12 a In this activity you have to name the notes in the pieces of music which have been written in bass clef.

Bach

  b What key is this piece of music in? _____

  c Out of the bassoon, trombone and cello, which instrument can play three notes at once as sometimes happens here? _____

  d So this piece of music is called Bourrée I from the Third Suite for _____

13 While the string family is playing the very famous 'Joy theme' (see below) in the Ninth Symphony by Beethoven, the bassoon plays this beautiful countermelody.

  a What is the line joining the two Gs over the barline called? _____

  b What key is this in? _____

  c What sort of rest appears in the last bar? _____

  d Write the note names on the spaces under the staff.

Beethoven

Discovering Musicianship Grade One 57

Unit Five

This is the opening of Sarastro's famous aria O Isis and Osiris from *The Magic Flute* by Mozart, the most performed of all operas.

Mozart

14 What key is this in? _____

   Write the note names on the spaces underneath the staff.

15 Which of these three themes has an anacrusis? _____

16 Write the scale degree numbers on top of the first two bars of each piece.

♪ Let Us Transpose!

How does a singer with a high voice sing the same song as someone with a low voice? How can a trumpet play the same melody as a double bass? How can two melodies be recognised as the same when they start, and continue, on different notes?

We shall begin our investigation with a little *Joy* from Beethoven.

17 **a** What key is this music in? _____

   b Write scale degree numbers under the first two bars of each one.

   c What did you discover? _____
   This is called **transposition**.

58   *Discovering Musicianship Grade One*

d On the staves below continue adding notes <u>an octave higher</u> as shown in the first bar. You will also notice that some dots need to be added to make the music rhythmically accurate.

e In the bass clef (below), add notes <u>an octave lower</u> in the first two bars. Then in the second two bars add notes an octave higher.
The first parts of both halves are done for you.

♪ New and Old Vocabulary

18 Match the words with their definition.

a	scale	1	A scale in western music that has three semitones
b	semitone	2	A rounded line connecting two or more notes telling the performer to play the notes under the line smoothly
c	key signature	3	The first degree of a scale; the keynote
d	harmonic minor scale	4	A line joining notes of the same pitch telling the performer to hold for the duration of both notes
e	major scale	5	The smallest interval in western music
f	slur	6	Sharps or flats placed at the beginning of each staff
g	tonic	7	The plural of staff
h	tie	8	Stepwise arrangement of notes
i	tone	9	A scale with semitones between degrees 3 & 4 , 7 & 8
j	staves	10	Two semitones

♪ Revision Worksheet Five

1. Add the missing barlines from these famous tunes. Two have anacruses. *Note*: these are just the openings and mostly do not end on the tonic.

   Bach

   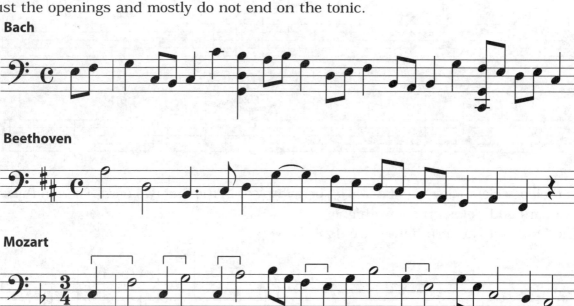

   Beethoven

   Mozart

   Schubert

   Grieg

2. **a** Name the notes in the melodies by Beethoven and Grieg.
   b Write scale degree numbers under the themes by Bach and Schubert.
   c Which theme finishes on its tonic? _____ (one only)
   d Which theme uses accidentals? _____ (one only)
   e Which themes have anacruses? _____ and _____

3. **a** Describe the key signature of the theme by Bach _____
   b What key is it in? _____
   c Write its scale here, firstly in the bass clef descending, then in the treble clef ascending. Mark the semitones with slurs.

Revision Worksheet Five

4 Name the intervals that are bracketed in the Mozart theme.

1 _____ 2 _____ 3 _____ 4 _____ 5 _____

5 **a** What is the key signature of the Schubert theme? _____

b What major key is it in? _____

c Write its scale here, one octave ascending _____
in the bass clef. Mark the semitones with
slurs.

6 Allegretto

a This theme (above) comes from Eine Kleine Nachtmusik

which is German for _____ _____ _____ _____.

It was composed by _____ (1756–91).

b What key is it in? _____ How many beats in a bar? _____

c Why are there only two beats in the last bar? _____

d What are the dots under the first notes called and what do they indicate?

_____

e What is the Italian term here indicating speed and what does it mean?

_____

f Write the scale degree numbers under the theme.

7 Transpose this melody up an octave to the pitch where the First Violins play it.
Do you know, or can you guess, what the other group of violins in an orchestra is called?

_____ _____

Remember to draw clefs, key signatures, the time signature and put in all barlines *before* drawing any notes. Then add other performance details.

Discovering Musicianship Grade One

Revision Worksheet Five

8 Write an F major scale in the bass clef scales using a key signature one octave descending. Write it in minims and mark the semitones with slurs.

9 Check with your teacher which tunes you should be learning to write out from memory. Write one of them from memory here. Include all performance details and words.

10 Complete these bars by adding *one* note at the end of each of them.

11 Complete these bars by adding *one* rest at the end of each of them.

62 *Discovering Musicianship Grade One*

Revision Worksheet Five

12 Match these verses and rhythms
   a Come all you young fellows, give an ear to my song
   b 'Twas on one Whitsun Wednesday, the fourteenth day of May
   c There was a sailor from Dover from Dover he came

13 a Which of these three tune beginnings have anacruses? _____
   b What key is the first tune in? _____ major.
   c What key is the second tune in? _____ major.

Discovering Musicianship Grade One

Welcome to Unit Six

In this unit we will

start working in minor keys
revise keys, scales and intervals
meet some relatives
discover the triad
do more with transposition

♪ Minor Scales

1 a A key signature of one sharp tells us that a piece of music is in ____ major. Sing or play this tune and you'll hear immediately that G is not the tonic and that it is not major.

b Can you name this tune? _____

Try to complete all the gaps below before checking your answers on page 99.

c What note does this tune start and finish on? _____

d As the last note is usually the key note or t __ __ __ __ , use it as 1 and write all the other notes in order.

64   Discovering Musicianship Grade One

e Circle the pairs of notes that form semitones. The semitones are between numbers ___ & ___ and ___ & ___.

f A major scale's semitones occur between ___ & ___ and ___ & ___. This scale is known as the **natural minor**. While there is only one type of major scale, there are several types of minor scales. The natural minor is typical in folk music and the **harmonic minor**, which we are about to study, is more common in classical music.

The Shearer's Dream

Most of the music we have seen so far in this course, with one sharp in the key signature, is in G major. This is not the case in *The Shearer's Dream*—have a look at the music below and write down two reasons this tune is different:

2   a _____

    b _____

3   Write the note names under the notes of the third and fourth staves.

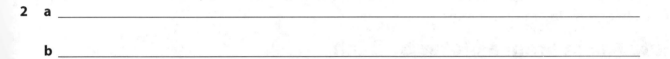

Unit Six

♪ Let's Discover the Minor Scale

4   **a Step One:** List, in alphabetical order, all the notes that are used in *The Shearer's Dream*. Given that E is the last note, we will use it as our first one here.

E ____ ____ ____ ____ ____ ____ ____

Don't forget the sharps!

  b Step Two: Circle the pairs of notes (letters) that are a *semitone* apart. While there are two pairs of semitones in a major scale, there are three in a harmonic minor scale. If you circled three pairs, you are on the right track. They are between the 2nd & 3rd and 5th & 6th and the 7th & 8th notes, that is between:

F♯ and ____   B and ____   D♯ and ____

  c Step Three: Write the numbers under the letters in Step One.
  Now we can see that Scale Degree number one (the tonic) is E. Therefore, the key of The Shearer's Dream is E minor.

Gute Nacht From a Motet by Bach

List all the notes used in the excerpt above. All excerpts are incomplete and some can finish on the tonic. We will have to work out the tonic from our knowledge of key signatures and semitones.

5   **a** Write here, in alphabetical order, all the notes that occur in this excerpt. Don't forget to include the sharp.   ____ ____ ____ ____ ____ ____ ____ ____

  b If there are two semitones it is probably a _____ scale.

  c If there are three semitones, it is probably a _____ scale. Where do the semitones occur in a minor scale? ____ & ____, ____ & ____, ____ & ____

  d Put a box around the interval of three semitones (tone and a half) which occurs between ____ & ____

  e You should now be able to write the scale degree numbers under this to find out the tonic. Write the tonic here: ____

  f There are two keys that have no sharps or flats in their key signature: ____ major and A minor. Do either of these come out as your solution?

  g Write the scale, one octave descending, in the treble clef and one octave ascending, in the bass.

♪ Keys and Scales Revisited

When you listen to music, you usually find that there is a note that seems to be the home note or key note. It is called the tonic.

6 Is it usually the first or last note of a melody? _____ We have already listed the notes used in a piece of music and created a scale for that piece. Let's do it again.

The Dying Stockman

Play this song and identify the tonic. Then list all the notes that are in it.

7 a Write these notes in order on the left stave starting from the tonic.
   b On the second stave write it again in the bass clef, descending from Middle C.

   c Do you remember the name for the curved lines connecting two notes of the same pitch? _____. It occurs four times in *The Dying Stockman*.
   d Why are there only two beats in the last bar? _____
   e If your scale has semitones between the 3rd and 4th notes and the 7th and 8th notes only, it is a ____ ____ ____ ____ ____ scale. Mark the semitones in these scales with slurs.

8 a Identify the major scale, the minor scale, and the two 'others'. Play them and listen to the differences.

Discovering Musicianship Grade One

Unit Six

Generally speaking:

b Are key signatures placed between the clef and the time signature? _____

c Are they on every staff or just the first one? _____

d What do they indicate? _____

♪ Relative Majors and Minors

9 a The pairs of notes on the staff below indicate the tonics of major and minor keys with the same key signatures. The first note is the tonic of the major key and the second is the tonic of the minor key. Write the names under them, for example, the last one tells us that two flats indicate B♭ major and G minor.

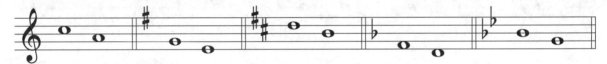

b Does this mean that two keys can have the same key signature? _____ Do you think this what is meant by 'relative'? _____

10 Circle the following true/false answers

a True/False   Every key signature can represent a major AND a minor key.

b True/False   Every key signature represents major keys only.

c True/False   By counting down three semitones from the major tonic, you arrive at the relative minor.

d True/False   The key signature of A minor is the same as D major's.

e True/False   The key signature of E minor is the same as G major's.

♪ Intervals Again

11 a When you name an interval, do you count the lower note as number one? _____

b Is this true in major and minor keys? _____

c Does an accidental affect the number of the interval? _____

d Name the intervals on the first stave below and write intervals above the given note on the second.

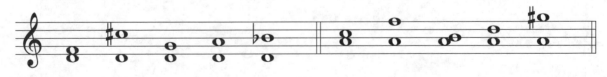

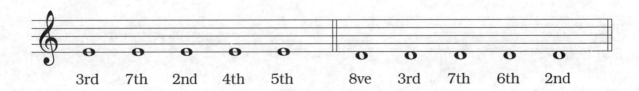

3rd   7th   2nd   4th   5th   8ve   3rd   7th   6th   2nd

68   *Discovering Musicianship Grade One*

♪ Triads

Just as most melodies end on the tonic, their accompaniment nearly always ends with the tonic triad.

But what's an accompaniment? And What's a tonic triad?

An **accompaniment** is the support given to a melody. On the piano the melody is often played by the right hand while the left hand accompanies it. A piano or orchestra can accompany a singer or a choir or a solo instrument.

12 On the lines under each each of these triads, write the interval number for the interval between:

a the bottom note and the middle note and
b the bottom note and the top note.

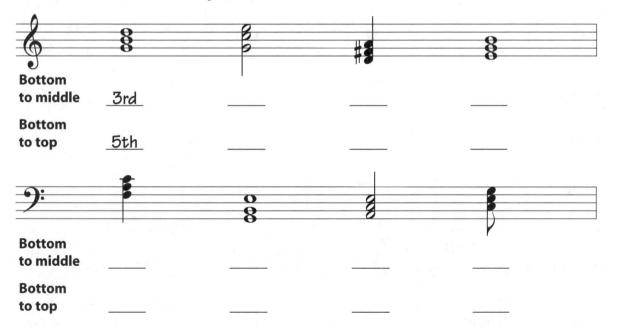

Bottom to middle   3rd   ____   ____   ____

Bottom to top   5th   ____   ____   ____

Bottom to middle   ____   ____   ____   ____

Bottom to top   ____   ____   ____   ____

c Which triads don't belong? Circle them, then write down what is different about them.

_____

Discovering Musicianship Grade One

Unit Six

Naming a Triad

A triad is named after the bottom note if there is a 3rd and 5th above it. It is **major** if the middle note is in the major scale of the bottom note. Read that again. And then write it out. Twice.

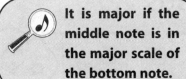
It is major if the middle note is in the major scale of the bottom note.

13 Name the triads, except for the ones you circled.

  a Treble clef: _____

  b Bass clef: _____

14 Name the upper and lower intervals on the lines below: the interval from the bottom note to the top note (the **upper interval**) and the interval from the bottom note to the middle (the **lower interval**).

Upper   ____   ____   ____   ____

Lower   ____   ____   ____   ____

Name   ____   ____   ____   ____

15 Identify these triads. Firstly name the intervals on the lines below.

Upper   ____   ____   ____   ____

Lower   ____   ____   ____   ____

Name   ____   ____   ____   ____

16 Compare these two examples (right). Play the notes either all at once, or one after the other.

  a What do you see? _____
  b What do you hear? _____
  c Which one is major? _____
  d Which is minor? _____

We noted earlier that the middle note had to be in the major scale if it's to be a major triad.

70   *Discovering Musicianship Grade One*

17 Firstly name the intervals. Then name the triads. They are all minor except one.

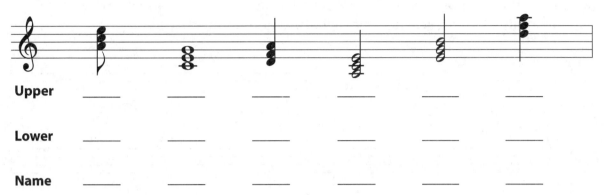

Upper	____	____	____	____	____	____
Lower	____	____	____	____	____	____
Name	____	____	____	____	____	____

18 True or False:
   a True/False   A minor triad has a higher middle note than a major triad.
   b True/False   The three notes in a major triad are in its major scale.
   c True/False   The three notes in a minor triad are in its minor scale.

Goe From My Window Goe

It is now time to put transposition to a much more practical use and transpose melodies. This melody is written at a suitable pitch for young people to sing and play on the recorder, the violin, the oboe, and so on but it is rather high for the cello.

19 Can you think of a woodwind or a brass instrument that plays at the same pitch as the cello? _____

20 a What key is the song in? _____
   b What does the time signature mean? _____
   c How many bars are there? _____
   d Which words or syllables have more than one note for them? _____
   e Which two pairs of bars are the same? _____ and _____
   f The interval from every note to the next note is a second (except for repeated notes) with three exceptions. Two are in bar ____ and the other is over the barline, from bar ____ to bar ____.
   g Name these three intervals. ____, ____ and ____.

Discovering Musicianship Grade One

Unit Six

21 On the staves below, transpose *Goe from My Window Goe* down one octave into the bass clef starting on the G below middle C (the fourth space in the bass clef). Be very careful with stem direction. Don't forget the time signature and double barline.

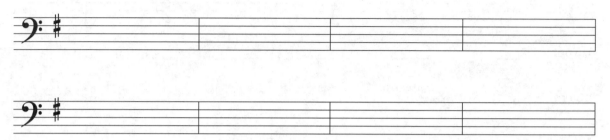

Robin Hood and the Curtal Friar

22 As usual, this is printed at a suitable pitch for people to sing or to play on the violin or oboe. But as you can see, there is a note in bar 6 which is out of range for flute and recorder. Their lowest note is Middle C. In order for them to be able to play the whole song, you will need to write it all up an octave.

Did you know that the notes that come out of a descant recorder are an octave higher than written?

72 *Discovering Musicianship Grade One*

Now answer the following questions on *Robin Hood and the Curtal Friar*.

23 a What key is the song in? _____

  b What does the time signature mean? _____

  c How many bars are there? _____

  d Which syllables have more than one note? _____

  e What is the interval between the first two notes? _____

  f In which two bars are there intervals of thirds? _____

  g Which bars do not have the tonic note in them? _____

> Start on D on the fourth line of the treble clef. And don't forget that most, if not all of your stems will come down since it is so high.

Le Cygne

Look at this wonderful melody by Camille Saint-Saëns (1835–1921) called *Le Cygne*. It comes from *The Carnival of the Animals*, a suite of pieces for small orchestra. You can guess from the picture what the English of *cygne* is: For further proof, what do we call its young in English? _____

Try playing this melody. If you listen to a recording of it you'll hear the serene accompaniment played on two pianos depicting the rippling water that the swan (cello) glides graciously across. It is played in the high part of the cello range. It therefore uses a lot of leger lines.

> The swan can swim while sitting down
> For pure conceit he takes the crown
> He looks in the mirror over and over
> And claims to have never heard of Pavlova.
> (Ogden Nash)

24 a Firstly, name the notes.

  b This melody could even also be played an octave lower on the cello. Transpose it. The first notes are done for you. Saint-Saëns wrote it in $\frac{6}{4}$, not a very common time signature.

  c Indicate where the **ties** and **slurs** are in this excerpt by writing these words onto the curved lines.

Unit Six

The Elephant

The next piece we are going to transpose down an octave is the pompous double bass solo, *The Elephant*, which also comes from *The Carnival of the Animals* by Camille Saint-Saëns. The notes that come out of a double bass sound one octave lower than written, as you can see below.

25 a How many flats are there in the key signature? ____

   b What three notes do they indicate are played as flats? ____ ____ ____

   c Circle all the notes that are played as flats.

   d Name all the notes in this opening phrase of *The Elephant*.

   e Rewrite the theme as it sounds, that is one octave lower.

Written like this

but sounds like this

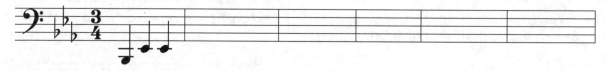

Same Pitch in Different Clefs

26 Find the starting notes on a keyboard.

Would you play these two phrases at the same pitch? ____

You can see that the first note in these two phrases is D, one tone/semitone above middle C. Does this mean that the two phrases start on the same note, even though they are in different clefs? ____

Revision Worksheet Six

1. Write a D minor scale one octave ascending in the treble clef and then in the bass clef. Use a key signature (and don't forget the accidental).

2. Write an E minor scale one octave ascending in the treble clef and the bass clef. Use a key signature (and accidentals where necessary).

3. All key signatures indicate major and minor keys. On the lines below the staff write the names of the major or minor keys that these key signatures represent. In the space beside each key signature, copy it very neatly.

   Major _____ _____ _____ _____

   Minor _____ _____ B minor _____

4. Name these triads.

5. Write these triads in the bass clef. Use accidentals where necessary.

   D major   E minor   F major   A minor   D minor   C major

Revision Worksheet Six

6 Write the scale degree numbers under this melody by Mozart and transpose it up one octave into the treble clef. Remember to set out the barlines before writing any notes.

7 What key is this melody by Bach in? _____

Does it finish on the tonic? _____

Is there an anacrusis? _____

Write the scale degree numbers above it and complete the transposition down one octave.

8 Name the intervals below and then rewrite them one octave lower in the bass clef.

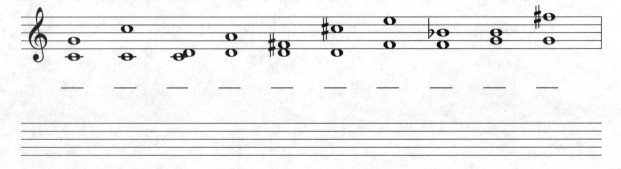

Revision Worksheet Six

9 a This is the beginning of the last movement of Beethoven's great Fifth Symphony. Add barlines. It is _____ bars long and is in _____ major.

b What does **ff** stand for and mean? _____

c What is the tempo marking and what does it mean?
_____

10 a This melody (below) comes from Mozart's Oboe Quartet. The key signature suggests _____ major but the C♯s suggest a minor key. What is it? _____.

b Add the time signature.

c If you can play it, can you hear whether it is major or minor?

d What does **Adagio** mean? _____

e What does **mf** stand for and indicate? _____

f What is the 'hairpin' line under the last two bars indicating? What is it called?
_____

g Write the names of the three bracketed intervals on the brackets. Remember that intervals are always counted from the lower note.

h Write the scale of this Mozart theme in the treble clef. Use a key signature and the accidental for the seventh degree. It should be one octave descending. Mark the three semitones with slurs.

Discovering Musicianship Grade One

Revision Worksheet Six

11 Mark the following statements as TRUE or FALSE.
   a True/False   A sharp raises a note one semitone
   b True/False   A flat raises a note one semitone
   c True/False   A tone consists of two semitones
   d True/False   An accidental adds half the value of a note to it
   e True/False   A *tempo* means to resume the original tempo
   f True/False   An accidental affects all notes of the same pitch for the rest of the piece
   g True/False   An accidental affects all notes of the same pitch for the rest of the bar
   h True/False   An accidental affects only the note it is attached to
   i True/False   An accidental is written on the left side of the note
   j True/False   An accidental is written on the right side of the letter name eg F#

12 Circle the notes that would be played sharp in the first melody, and flat in the second one.

13 Do you remember learning about the dot? Go back to page 17 if you need help remembering then complete the following activities.
   a Add one dot only to each of these bars to make it complete.

   b Add one rest to complete each of these bars. One dotted rest will be needed.

14 Write a rhythm for the following couplet.

As I walked out one morn in May, The birds did sing and the lambs did play

Welcome to Unit Seven

In this unit we will

go through all the keys that
you need to know in First Grade
revise rhythm
  beat, time signature, accents, anacrusis,
  barlines, rests, the dot
and pitch
  notes, treble, bass, leger lines,
  clefs, keys, intervals, triads
and vocabulary
and transposition
and notation

In this final unit, you are required to go through the Grade's keys and songs in a variety of ways. You should really know it all then.

♪ C Major

1 a Write the names of some music in C major that you have met in this book, you should be able to find at least five.

_____

b On the stave below, write a C major scale, two octaves ascending in the bass clef starting two leger lines below the staff. Mark the semitones with slurs.

c Write the tonic triad and the intervals indicated above Middle C in the treble clef.

      Tonic Triad   3rd   4th   5th   8ve   2nd

Discovering Musicianship Grade One

Unit Seven

Ave Maria

2 a Transpose this famous *Ave Maria* by Charles Gounod down an octave. The barlines are missing so you'll have to put them in first.

Charles Gounod wrote this *Ave Maria* as a composition exercise. Students were asked to write a melody over the famous C major Prelude by Bach. Apparently a friend of his rushed out and had it published much to Gounod's anger.

Answer the following questions about *Ave Maria*.

b **Andante** means _____

c *Cantabile* means in a singing style. The Italian word for 'sing' is *cantare*

   cresc is short for _____ and means _____

   p is short for _____ and means _____

   pp is short for _____ and means _____

d Identify the slurs here by writing **slur** on them. How many are there? _____

e Identify the ties by writing **tie** on them. How many are there? _____

f There is one rest in this excerpt. What is it? _____

   What value does it have? _____

g What does *Ave Maria* mean? _____

♪ A Minor

3 a Write an A minor scale in the treble clef in semibreves.
Write it descending and ascending without a break and without repeating the bottom note.
Mark the semitones with slurs and write the scale degree numbers underneath.
Start on the first leger line above the staff. At the end of the staff, write the tonic triad.

In a question with so many parts, it is a good idea to underline each bit to make sure you have understood all the requirements.

In 1738–42, Bach wrote two books of Preludes and Fugues. The first Preludes and Fugues are in C major. The second in C minor, the third in C♯ major, the fourth in C♯ minor. See the pattern? He wrote for every note.

> **b** If you like quizzes of logic you might like to work out how many Preludes and Fugues there are in each book.
>
> **c** This is the beginning of the Fugue in A minor. Write it an octave higher in the treble clef. Then circle the four beats per bar.

♪ G Major

4 a How do we know that *Goe from my Window Goe*, on page 71, is in G major?

> **b** Write a G major scale in the treble clef in crotchets, taking care of stem direction. Use the key signature. Write it ascending and descending without a break and without repeating the top note. Start on the second line of the staff. At the end of the staff, write the tonic triad of G major.
>
> **c** Write intervals in G major, with a key signature. Always count up. The required note will always be ABOVE the tonic.

    3rd   5th   7th   8ve   2nd   4th   6th

Discovering Musicianship Grade One

Unit Seven

Eine Kleine Nachtmusik

d All of these opening bars of Mozart's very famous Eine Kleine Nachtmusik are incomplete. Complete them with rests (under the asterisks). On the staff below, transpose it down an octave.

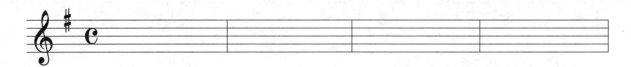

♪ E Minor

5 a What is the Australian folk song in E minor that we worked with in the last unit?

_____

b On the stave below, write the scale of E minor, one octave descending in the treble clef with a key signature. Write it in minims and mark the semitones with slurs.

c Write the tonic triad and these intervals above E.

        Tonic Triad   6th   4th   7th   8ve   2nd

6 This is an excerpt from Beethoven's Piano Sonata No 9. There are rests missing (under the asterisks) which you should add. You should fill the empty bars (9 to 14) with a transposition of bars 1 to 6 up an octave.

82   *Discovering Musicianship Grade One*

Anacrusis Revision

7 Read this verse aloud while tapping the beat. Underline the first accented syllable in every line—you will notice that every line has an anacrusis. Add barlines—there are four per line. The first one has been done for you.

On a | summer day in the month of May

Once a hobo was a hiking

Down a shady lane thru the sugar cane

He was looking for his liking.

♪ F Major

8 a Write an F major scale in the treble clef in crotchets taking care of stem direction. Use the key signature. Write it ascending and descending without a break and without repeating the top note.

Start on the bottom space of the staff. At the end of the staff, write the tonic triad of F major.

b Write these intervals in F major in the bass clef. Do not use a key signature. Use the F below the staff as the bass note for the intervals.

    3rd   6th   5th   7th   8ve   2nd   4th

9 a Here are the words to the first verse of a not very well-known Australian folk song, *Look Out Below!* Like most Australian folk songs, it is anacrusic. Put the barlines in before the accented syllables. Then, in two syllable words, underline the syllables separately.

A young man left his native town

Through trade being slack at home

To seek his fortune in this land

He crossed the briny foam.

Discovering Musicianship Grade One

Unit Seven

b Here is the tune of *Look Out Below*. You should add dots to complete some of the bars. Under the notes, write in the appropriate words or syllables.

The slurs indicate that one syllable is sung on the two notes, for example the second slur has 'he' being sung on two notes.

c Now transpose the tune up an octave so that a flute could play along with it. The low B♭ is out of range for the flute.

♪ D Minor

10 a Look through the whole book and name some music that appears in D minor.

b Write the scale of D minor, one octave ascending in semibreves. Mark the semitones with slurs.

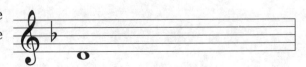

84 *Discovering Musicianship Grade One*

c Write the scale of D minor, one octave descending. Use minims and accidentals. Mark the semitones with slurs.

d Write the tonic triad and the intervals indicated above D. Use accidentals and write in the treble cleft.

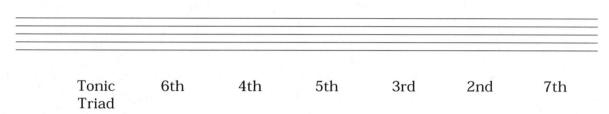

Tonic Triad   6th   4th   5th   3rd   2nd   7th

Minuet in D Minor

11 a The first four bars of a Bach's Minuet in D Minor follow. Because the leading note (the seventh note in a scale) has not been raised, it is in the natural minor. However, Bach wrote it in the harmonic minor, so you'll need to raise all the sevenths in this phrase.
  b Then you should label the staves and musical notation.
  c Finally, you should write the scale degree numbers under the right hand melody, and the note names under the left hand part.

♪ D Major

12 a Write a D major scale in the treble clef in minims taking care of stem direction. Use the key signature. Write it ascending and descending without a break and without repeating the top note.

Unit Seven

b Write the tonic triad and these intervals in D major in the bass clef. Use a key signature.

| Tonic Triad | 6th | 3rd | 8ve | 2nd | 7th | 5th |

Violin Concerto

13 To this theme from Beethoven's Violin Concerto you should firstly add barlines and then transpose it down an octave into the bass clef. Remember to set out the clefs and barlines first.

At the beginning write a tempo mark that means *lively and fast* and a dynamic mark indicating *soft*.

Revision Worksheet Seven

1 **a** Add a clef and accidentals to make a scale of D major.
   b Mark the semitones

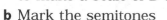

2 **a** Turn back to page 46 and write the note names under the notes of the Allegretto.
   b Turn back to page 82 and do the same with Eine Kleine Nachtmusik

3 **a** Complete the following bars with quavers correctly grouped.

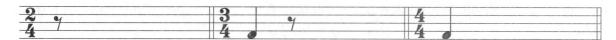

   b What time signature do the following single bars require?

4 Add words and signs to God Rest Ye Merry Gentlemen on page 64 to show the following:
   a It should be lively and fast.
   b It should slow down at the end.
   c It should start moderately loud.
   d The third phrase (around bars 9–12) should be smooth.
   e The last three bars should get louder.

5 Name the intervals.

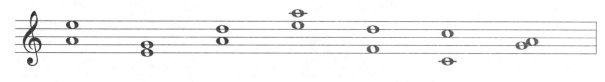

6 **a** Turn back to page 63 and write the scale degree numbers under the notes of the first two melodies.
   b Transpose the third melody on page 63 up an octave.

7 Write the following triads in the bass clef.

   C major   D minor   A minor   F major   G major

Discovering Musicianship Grade One

Revision Worksheet Seven

8 Place an upright line before each accented word or syllable.

   a Chase my mouse around the house but please don't rouse you rotten louse.

   b Waiting for someone to come to the sunroom
   I opened the mail that had come from the gaol.

   c Thoughts of you are always near;
   hurry home my dearest dear.
   What a shame you're far away;
   How I miss you every day.

9 Write out one of the set pieces from memory. Do not forget to space the words properly and remember to include all performance details. Choose the one that you find the most challenging, or let your teacher choose one for you.

Glossary

Accent An emphasis given to a note, usually by playing it more loudly. Signs include: > and ∧.

Accidental A sharp (♯), flat (♭) or natural (♮) is used in a piece of music to indicate a change to what the key signature requires.

Accompaniment This typically refers to what the piano plays when playing with other musicians.

Anacrusis An unstressed note, or group of notes, at the beginning of a phrase of music that forms an upbeat.

Bass Clef The sign placed at the beginning of staves to indicate lower pitches. Because it centres around the line for F, it has also been known as an F clef.

Beam The line connecting the tops of stems of quavers and semiquavers.

Canon see Round

Chamber Music Music written for a small group of instruments, originally intended for performance in a small room, hence chamber. The names given to these small groups are: 1. Solo 2. Duo 3. Trio 4. Quartet 5. Quinete 6. Sextet 7. Septet 8. Octet 9. Nonet

Common Time The most common time signature is 4/4 and is often indicated by 𝄵 instead of 4/4.

Composer A person who writes music.

Concerto A piece of music written for a solo instrument accompanied by an orchestra. The most common instrument that concertos are written for are the violin and the piano.

Crotchet A rhythmic value also known as a quarter note. Four crotchets make a semibreve.

Dot When written beside a note, it adds half the value of the note to the note. A dotted minim therefore has three beats: two from the minim and one from the dot, one being half of two.

Double Barline Two vertical lines cutting through a stave to show the end of a section or a piece.

Dynamics The umbrella term for loudness and softness and changes from loud to soft etc. in music.

Excerpt A part of a piece of music.

Flat One of the three accidentals. This sign (♭) tells the player to play a semitone lower than the note would be without it. It can appear as an accidental or in the key signature.

Folk song A type of song usually associated with rural areas, with peasants and with music passed on orally from generation to generation.

Harmonic minor The form of the minor that contains an interval of three semitones. In A minor, for example, it is from F to G♯. This, more than anything, gives the harmonic minor its individual sound.

Interval The distance in pitch from one note to another. For example, from C to G is a fifth; from A to C is a third.

Key The key of a piece of music is shown by its key signature. With very few exceptions, the last note of a piece is the same as the key.

Discovering Musicianship Grade One

Glossary

Keyboard The black and white notes on pianos, organs, etc., form the keyboard. Many modern electric instruments with keyboards are often referred to simply as 'keyboards'.

Key signature The sharps or flats at the beginning of each stave of music are the key signature for the piece or the section.

Leger lines Short, horizontal lines written above and below the staff on which notes are written when the pitch is outside the range of the staff.

Major The most common type of key, the other being minor. Major keys have seven notes and when arranged as a scale, there are semitones between the 3rd and 4th notes and the 7th and 8th.

Melody Also known as a tune. It is an arrangement of notes in a certain rhythm usually with a beginning, middle and end.

Metronome This machine was designed to indicate the tempo (speed) of a piece of music.

Minor The second most common type of key. There are various minors but they all have a minor third between the tonic and the third note.

Middle C This is the note on the first leger line below the treble staff and on the first leger line above the bass staff. On a piano, it is right in the middle of the keyboard.

Minim A rhythmic value also known as a half note. Two minims make a semibreve. The word is a palindrome.

Minuet An elegant dance in $\frac{3}{4}$, at a moderate tempo.

Motif A short phrase of music that is played frequently during a piece of music, often in different ways.

Natural One of the three accidentals. This sign (♮) tells the player not to play the note as a sharp or a flat as is indicated by the key signature. For example a composer of a piece of music in F major might want B♮ sometimes. Since B♭ is in the key signature, it must be cancelled, and this is what the natural does.

Natural minor The form of the minor that is more common in folk music than composed music. It does not have a semitone between the 7th and 8th degrees of the scale and this makes it different from both harmonic minor and major keys.

Octave The interval or distance, higher or lower, between eight notes or steps, where you reach a note with the same letter name. For example: C to C—(see Scale).

Pause (⌒) A sign placed over a note telling the performer to hold the note longer than its value indicates. The length in this case depends on the taste of the performer.

Pianoforte The full name for the piano. *Piano* is the Italian word for soft and *forte* for loud. The instrument was so called because the instrument could play loud and soft according to the pianist's touch.

Phrase A section of a melody. Several of these usually make a melody. When sung or played on wind instruments, a phrase typically lasts for one breath.

Pitch The highness and lowness of sound. Pitch is the umbrella term covering notes names, sharps, clefs, keys, scales, etc.

Prelude A piece of music that is complete in itself but serves to introduce a larger piece.

Quartet see Chamber music

Glossary

Quaver A rhythmic value also known as an eighth note. Eight quavers make a semibreve.

Repeat Play a section of music again. This is indicated by a double barline with two dots in front of it.

Rest A period of silence or the sign for a period of silence.

Rhythm The umbrella term covering time in music: the duration of notes and beat. It does not cover tempo.

Round Also known as canon. Refers to the singing of a melody when one singer begins, another joins in with the same melody a little later, another does the same.

Scale The alphabetical arrangement of all the note names that belong to a key. For example, F major: F G A B♭ C D E F.

Scale degree number Every note is a numerical distance from the tonic or keynote. For example, the note B in D major is 6 and C in F major is 5.

Semiquaver A rhythmic value also known as a sixteenth note. Sixteen semiquavers make a semibreve.

Sharp One of the three accidentals. This sign (♯) tells the player to play a semitone higher than the note would be without it. It can appear as an accidental or in the key signature.

Slur A curved line linking two or more notes telling the player to play the notes smoothly, that is, without breaks between them.

Staff/Stave The set of five lines that music is written on.

Stem The vertical line attached to a note head. All notes have stems except semibreves.

Syllable One unit of sound in a word. *Slur* has one syllable, *tempo* has two, *symphony* three, *semiquaver* four.

Symphony A composition for orchestra consisting of four separate sections called movements. It has been the standard form of orchestral composition since the mid 18th century.

Tail The wavy line at the end of the stem of quavers and semiquavers.

Theme A melody that a composer uses repeatedly during a composition. Being a complete melody, it is longer than a motif.

Tie A curved line linking two or more notes of the same pitch telling the player to hold the first note for the duration of all the notes linked.

Time Signature The numbers that appear at the beginning of a piece of music or section indicating what type of beat the piece has (the lower number) and how many of them there are in a bar (the upper number).

Tone The quality of a musical sound. This refers to the difference that can be heard when a trumpet plays and when a violin or flute plays.

Transposition When a melody is transposed, it is rewritten in a higher or lower key.

Treble clef The sign placed at the beginning of staves to indicate higher pitches. Because it centres around the line for G, it has also been known as a G clef.

Triad Three notes, usually played together, formed by adding the third and fifth notes above the bottom (bass) note. For example, the triad on C is C E G and on G is G B D.

Trio see Chamber music

Tune see Melody

Answers to Unit One

1. (a) There are 88. (b) Yes. Higher notes could be added to the piano. So could lower notes. The highest and lowest possible note depends on your hearing. (c) There are seven. (d) A B C D E F G. (e) You start again. The note after G is always A. (f) To the left of two black notes is C. (g) To the left of three black notes is F.
2. First note on the left of the keyboard is C. Then D E F G A B then the C that is already shown. Then D E F G A B C.
3. (a) It winds around the second line from the bottom. (b) It crosses on the fourth line from the bottom.
4. (a) Five. (b) Four. (c) Nine. Note that the plural of staff is staves. The singular 'stave' can also be used instead of the word 'staff'. (d) The spaces from bottom to top are <u>F A C E</u>. The standard mnemonic is **<u>Every Good Boy Deserves Fruit</u>**. (e) You will notice that there are two Es and Fs.
5. (a) E G B D F; F A C E. (b) E F G A B C D E F
6. (a) E G B F D G E F B. (b) A F C E F E A C E
7. (a) E F G A B C D E F; (b) E and F.
8. (a) F E E F D G F A E B C D. (b) B G A F E D E E B D F C
10. G, so the treble clef is also known as the G Clef.
11. a = 3; b = 4; c = 5; d = 7; e = 8; f = 2; g = 6; h = 1
12. a = 5; b = 3; c = 6; d = 1; e = 8; f = 4; g = 7; h = 2
13.
14. (a) B G F D F B E G F E; (b) F G B D F E G E F D;
    (c) A E F C E A F E A C; (d) F A A E C F E A C F;
    (e) F D E C E G A B F D; (f) F E B F A E D E F A
15. (a) The semibreve is an oval on its side. (b) The minim's note head is basically the same shape. (c) Stems are on the right side going up and on the left side going down. (d) Semiquaver Tails point right whether the stem is up or down. (e) Their noteheads are like the crotchet's. (f) Beams are thicker than stems. Upward stems are on the right. Downward stems are on the left. (g) Semiquaver beams are equal thickness.
16. Notes above the middle line of the stave have downward stems and those below the middle line have upward stems. A note on the middle line can go up or down, depending on what the stems before and after it are doing.

Answers to Unit Two

1. (a) There are 88 notes on the keyboard. (b) D E F. (c) D E F G A B C D. (d) G F E. (e) G F E D C B A G
2. (a) E D C B A G (this G is the violin's lowest note) F G A B C. (b) A D C A E G C F B B G
3. (a) C D A D F G G A A C. (b) C A G E D F A D E D.
   (c) G A F F D A G D E A. (d) C A B B A G E E G G.
   (e) F G A B C E D C B A. (f) C B A G F F F A C D.
   (g) F A D E A B A C A G
4. (see grid)
5. (a) Semibreve; (b) Minim; (c) Crotchet;
   (d) Quaver; (e) Four crotchets; (f) two crotchets;
   (g) one crotchet; (h) half a crotchet.
6. (a) **Stems:** crotchet, quaver, minim. (b) **Tails:** quaver, semiquaver.
   (c) **Filled in:** crotchet, quaver, semiquaver. (d) **Not filled in:** semibreve.
7. (a) There are 4 quavers in a minim and 4 crotchets in a semibreve.
   (b) There are 2 crotchets in a minim and 8 quavers in a semibreve.
   (c) There are 2 quavers in a crotchet and 2 minims in a semibreve.
8.

Bar	First note in the bar	Last note in the bar	Sum of the values	Note name
a	crotchet	crotchet	4 crotchets	F
b	quaver	crotchet	5 crotchets	C
c	minim	quaver	4 crotchets	G
d	semibreve	crotchet	7 crotchets	G
e	minim	crotchet	9 crotchets	B
f	quaver	minim	8 crotchets	E

9. Half a circle, half a quaver. Yes, a semibreve is half a breve. Breves are hardly used at all these days. But in the earliest days of writing down music there were notes only for long and short. These were called the *longa* and *breve*.

10

		1	2	3	4
	There should be **four** beats in a bar.				
a	How many beats in this bar?	3	3½	3½	3
b	How much is missing?	1	½	½	1
c	Draw one note that would complete this bar.	♩	♪	♪	♩

11

		1	2	3	4
a	How many beats in each bar?	3½	3½	3	3½
b	What is missing?	♪	♪	♩	♪

12 (a) semibreve 4 dotted semibreve: 4 + 2 = 6. (b) minim 2 dotted minim: 2 + 1 = 3.
(c) crotchet 1 dotted crotchet: 1 + ½ = 1½

13 A dot has half the value of the note it belongs with.

14

15 (a) The first. (b) It is always the first beat after the barline.

16 (a) A time signature is written only at the beginning of a piece unless it changes during the piece. (b) It is not written at the beginning of every staff as a key signature is.

17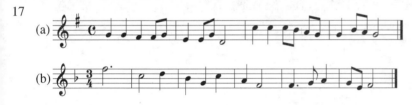

18 (a) Mozart 3/4. (b) Bach 4/4.

19

20

21 It tells the performer how many beats there are in a bar **and** what type of beats they are. It does **not** show speed.

22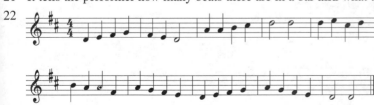

Clue—the time signature is 4/4.

23

24

Speed	Speed Changing	Volume	Other
moderato	rallentando	mezzo piano	legato
allegro	ritardando	diminuendo	staccato

Answers to Unit Three

1. (a) A sharp is one semitone <u>higher</u> than a note with the same letter name. The sound is <u>higher</u> and the direction on the keyboard is to the <u>right</u>. (b) A flat is one step <u>lower</u> than a note with the same letter name. The sound is <u>lower</u> and the direction on the keyboard is to the <u>left</u>.

   (d)

Black note number	Sharp name	Flat name
1 and 6	C♯	D♭
2 and 7	D♯	E♭
3 and 8	F♯	G♭
4 and 9	G♯	A♭
5 and 10	A♯	B♭

   They are written on the left on the staff and on the right with letter names. (e) F♯ C♯ G♯ B♭ E♭ A♭ C D A.

2. (a) There are two sharps in this song. (b) They are F♯ and C♯. (c) The last note is D.

   (d)

3. (a) The flat in the key signature is B♭. (b) The last note is F.

   (c)

4. C = B♯; C♯ = D♭; D♯ = E♭; E = F♭; F♯ = G♭; G♯ = A♭; A♯ = B♭.

5. (c) An accidental lasts for the rest of the bar it is in.

6. (a)

   (b) On the left of notes. (c) On the right of letter names.

7.

8 (a) Yes. It must be. (b) Melody 1: 1 5 | 5 6 5 3 | 2 4 3 2 2 | 1 |.
   (b) Melody 2: 1 1 3 3 | 5 6 5 4 3 2 1 | 1 5 3 | 4 3 1 |.
9 (a) G is 1, A is 2, B is 3, C is 4, D is 5, E is 6, F♯ is 7, G is 8. (b & c) Yes. It must be.
10 Tallis' Canon | 1 1 7 1 | 2 2 3 1 | 4 4 3 3 | 2 2 1 5 | 4 2 3 3 | 2 2 1 5 | 6 7 1 3 | 2 2 1 |.
11 (a) In F major, F is 1, G is 2, A is 3, B♭ is 4, C is 5, D is 6, E is 7, F is 8.
   (b)

   (c) Yes.
12 5 3 5 | 5 3 5 | 6 5 4 3 | 2 3 4 | 5 1 1 1 1 | 1 2 3 4 5 | 5 2 2 4 | 3 2 1 |
13 (a) E to F is a second. (b) F to C is a fifth. (c) A to F is a sixth. (d) B to G is a sixth. (e) D to A is a fifth.
14 (a) 1 tone = 2 semitones. A **semi**tone is **half** a tone. (b) G to A has a note in between, whereas B to C has none. Therefore G to A consists of two semitones and B to C is one semitone. (c) The two types of seconds are tone and semitone. (d) Two semitones make a TONE. No note between—a semitone. The smallest interval—a semitone. (e) You boxed G♯ - A and B - C. You circled F - G♯ because there are two notes between F and G♯.
15 C C C D | C C G | A G A B | C C | C C C D | C C G | A G A B | C C |
   G F E D | E D C | A G A B | C C | G G A B | C C D | G F E D | C F | C ||
   Step One: C D E F G A B C
   Step Two: You circled E & F, B & C. You can say that again: semitones are between the 3rd and 4th notes and the 7th and 8th notes in a major scale.
   You have probably already realised that 1 and 8 are the same note (but in different octaves)!
   Step Three: Yes, 1 is the last note in the piece and the tonic.
16 Step One: C♯ then D E F♯ G A B
   Step Two: You circled F♯ & G, C♯ & D.
   Step Three: Yes it does.
17 (b) 3 & 4, 7 & 8. (c) C major. (d) F major. (e) No it is not.
18 a = 10; b = 6; c = 5; d = 1; e = 2; f = 12; g = 4; h = 3; i = 8; j = 14; k =11; l = 7; m = 9; n = 13.

Answer to Unit Four

1 (a) 88. (b) 9, 2, 11. (c) 22.
2 (a) The traditional mnemonic is: <u>Good Boys Deserve Fruit Always</u>.
  (b) The spaces from bottom to top are A C E G—<u>All Cows Eat Grass</u>.
3 (a) D F G E A C A B G G. (b) Notes above the middle line have <u>downward</u> stems. Notes below have <u>upward</u> stems. And notes on the middle line can go either up or down, depending on the nearby notes.

   (c)

4 (a) D G B A F D G F A G. (b) F D B A G F B D G A.
  (c) A G E A G C E G A C. (d) G C E G A G E A C E.
  (e) G A F D E G B C F A. (f) A G D E A B G F G D.
  (g) E D C F A G A B A G. (h) F G G A A F E D C G.
5 (a) Descending: count <u>backwards</u>. (b) Ascending: count <u>forwards</u>.
  (c) G F E D C G A B C D.

   (d)

   (e) C F E C G B E A D D B
6 (a) E F | G C B C C | [G D B] A B G D E |
   F B A B G | [C G F] E D E C |
   (b) C major
   (c) 3 4 | 5 1 7 1 1 (8) | 5 2 7 6 7 5 2 3 | 4 7 6 7 5 | 1 5 4 3 2 3 1 |

7

8   (a) F G A B C G F E D C. (b) F A C E G B C A F E. (c) C E G B D F A C B A. (d) D F A C E G B C C C.
    (e) C E D E D F G A B C. (f) A C E D G A B F A C. (g) C A B C D E F D G C. (h) C A B D F A A B C D.
9   (a) 4; Oblong; It hangs from the fourth line. (b) 2; Oblong; It sits on the third line.
    (c) 1; From the top. (d) ½; From the top; No it's on an angle. (e) ¼; Yes, you do. (f) The semibreve rest.
10 A = 4, B = 5, C = 2, D = 3, E = 1.
11
(a)

(b)

(c) The top staff is in F major and it is in common time. The second one is in G major. The time signature is ¾.

12 (a)

(b) G to B = 3rd; G to D = 5th; G to F# = 7th; G to A = 2nd; G to C = 4th; G to E = 6th

(c)

(d) F to B♭ = 4th; F to D = 6th; F to G = 2nd; F to A = 3rd; F to C = 5th; F to E = 7th
(e) A 4th above D = G; A 5th above D = A; An 8ve above D = D; A 6th above D = B; A 7th above D = C#;
A 3rd above D = F#
(f) 4th, 7th, 6th, 5th, 2nd, 5th, 8ve, 4th, 6th, 3rd

(g)

13 (a) F major = one flat B♭. (b) F. (c) F major. (d) F. (e) Common time (4/4)

(f)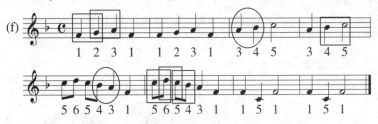

(g) crotchet rest (𝄽), minim rest (➖), quaver rest (𝄾).

Answers to Unit Five

1   1 roamed, 4 enviable, 3 wonderful, 1 style, 2 crotchet,
    3 thankfully, 2 minim, 1 stream, 2 zany, 2 tiger
    2 trumpet, 3 barrister, 2 wicked, 3 Iowa, 1 it
    2 keyboard, 2 trundle, 3 comedy, 3 daffodil, 3 overcoat

2   (a) & (b) One syllable: roamed, stream, style, it.
    Two syllables: <u>wick</u>-ed, <u>trum</u>-pet, <u>key</u>-board, <u>min</u>-im, <u>trun</u>-dle, <u>zan</u>-y, <u>crotch</u>-et, <u>ti</u>-ger.
    Three syllables: <u>won</u>-der-ful, <u>thank</u>-ful-ly, <u>bar</u>-ris-ter, <u>com</u>-e-dy, <u>I</u>-o-wa, <u>daff</u>-o-dil, <u>o</u>-ver-coat.
    Four syllables: <u>en</u>-vi-a-ble.
    (c) True. All of these words do have the first syllable accented.

3   (a) & (b) Two syllables: Accented first: mount-ain, par-rot; Accented second: re-duce, pa-rade.
    Three syllables: Accented first: na-tion-al, e-le-phant; Accented second: al-leg-ro, un-fin-ished;
    Accented third: tam-bour-ine, cock-a-too.
    Four syllables: Accented first: cir-cum-stanc-es, diff-i-cult-y; Accented second: mus-ic-ian-ship, pho-to-graph-er;
    Accented third: rall-en-tan-do, trans-pos-it-ion.

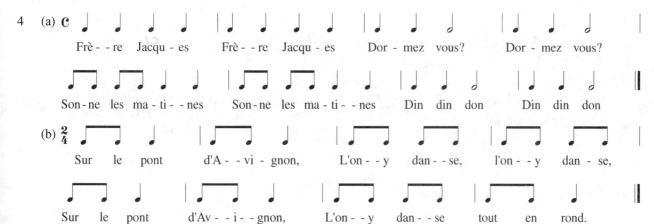

5   (a) This Old Man: A | A | F | A | E | B | F | A ‖
    Hot Cross Buns: A | A | C | A | D | B | C | A ‖

6   (a) In | sum-mer time when leaves grow green (b) | Un-to us is born a Son (c) I | had a little nut tree
    (d) A | far-mer's son so sweet (e) | Lav-en-der's blue dil-ly dil-ly (f) The | hol-ly and the i-vy
    (g) My | name is Bob the swag-man (h) One | night when trav-'ling sheep (i) Then | blow ye winds heigh ho!
    (j) My | bon-nie lies over the o-cean (k) Oh | Shen-an-doah I long to hear you

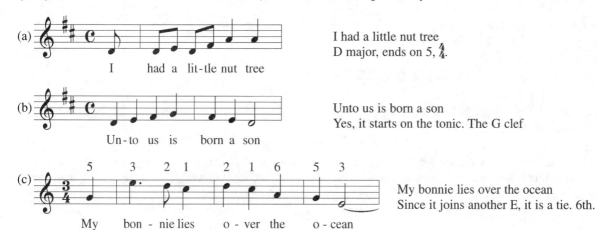

Discovering Musicianship Grade One

(c)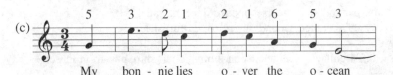

My bonnie lies over the ocean
Since it joins another E, it is a tie. 6th.

(d)

Lavender's blue dilly dilly
Three beats in a bar. 5th.

(e)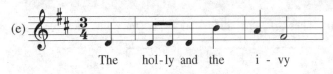

The holly and the ivy
The first, third and fifth excerpts have less than a full bar before the first full bar.

8 I had a little nut tree, My bonnie lies over the ocean, The holly and the ivy.

9

10 Here are the upright lines for the five that you ticked:
Au-|-stralians let us all rejoice,
Oh | come,
On | top of,
My | bonnie lies,
There | was an old man.
Your upright line went **before** the first word in the other songs.

11

12 (a) E F | G C B C C | [G D B] A B G D E | F B A B G | [C G F] E D E C |
(b) The Bach is in C major. (c) Cello. (d) It is a cello suite.

13 (a) The line is a tie. (b) The Beethoven is in D major. (c) The example ends with a crotchet rest.
(d) A D | B C♯ D G | G F♯ E D C♯ B A | G A F♯ |

14 The Mozart is in F major.
C | F C | G C | A B♭ G | F E G | B♭ G | D G D | C B♭ | A |

15 The Bach and Mozart are anacrusic.

16 Bach—SDN: 3 4 | 5 1 7 1 8 | 7 6 7 5 2 3 |
Beethoven—SDN: 5 1 | 6 7 8 4 |
Mozart—SDN: 5 | 1 5 | 2 5 |

17 (a) It is in D major and so D = 1. (b) SDN: 3 3 4 5 5 4 3 2 for each one. (c) That although they are at different pitches, they have the same SDN's and are therefore the same melody but in different octaves. (d) If there is more than one note on a stem, and it is a dotted note, every note has to be dotted, not just one of them.

18 a = 8, b = 5, c = 6, d = 1, e = 9, f = 2, g = 3, h = 4, i = 10, j = 7.

Answers to Unit Six

1 (a) G. (b) The song is God Rest Ye Merry Gentlemen. (c) It starts and finishes on E. (d) As the last note is usually the key note or **TONIC**: E F♯ G A B C D E (semitones are underlined). (e) The semitones are between numbers 2 & 3 and 5 & 6. (f) A major scale's semitones occur between 3 & 4 and 7 & 8. The very important difference between the **harmonic** and **natural** minors is the semitone between 7 & 8.

2 (a) It doesn't end on G. (b) D♯ frequently appears. Notice also that it is in a fairly prominent position, near the end of a phrase.

3 A A A B C B G E E A A A B C B B B B
   E B B A B G E E E F♯ G F♯ E B D♯ E E

4 (a) E F♯ G A B C D♯ E (b) F♯ and G, B and C, D♯ and E. (c) 1 2 3 4 5 6 7 1

5 (a) E F G♯ A B C D. (Your answer might not start on E. But it should have the same notes and be in order). (b) Major scale. (c) Minor scale. Semitones in the minor: 2 & 3, 5 & 6, 7 & 8. (d) Tone and half between 5 & 6. (e) The tonic is A. (f) Only C major and A minor have no sharps or flats in their key signatures.

6 While the tonic can be the first note of a melody, it nearly always is the last.

7

(c) The lines are called TIES. If they connect notes of **different** pitches, they are slurs. (d) The last bar has only two beats because of the anacrusis. (e) It is a major scale.

8 (a) The first scale is G major, the semitones coming between B and C, F♯ and G. The second is D minor with semitones between E and F, A and B♭, C♯ and D. On the second staff, the five note scale has no semitones. (b) Yes—between the clef and time signature. (c) They are on every staff—it is the time signature that is on the first staff only. (d) Key signatures indicate the flats or sharps to play and the key of the piece.

9 (a) C major & A minor, G major & E minor, D major & B minor, F major & D minor. (b) Yes, two keys can have the same signature. This is what is meant by 'relative'.

10 (a) true. (b) false. (c) true. (d) false. (e) true.

11 (a) Yes. (b) Yes. (c) No. (d) 3rd, 7th, 4th, 5th, 6th. | 3rd, 6th, 2nd, 4th, 7th.

Important note: E to D and E to D♯ are different types of 7ths, which means both answers are correct. The same is true of E to F♯, D to C♯ and D to B♭. The accidentals are optional when answering a question concerning the number of an interval.

12 (a) **Treble clef:** Triad on G—4rd and 6th. Triad on D—3rd and 5th. Triad on E—3rd and 5th.
    (b) **Bass clef:** Triad on F—3rd and 5th. Triad on G—3rd and 6th. Triad on A—3rd and 5th. Triad on C—3rd and 5th.
    (c) You circled the second triad on both staves because they don't consist of a 3rd and a 5th. Please note that it is different, **not** wrong. The circled triads do have a special place in music. They are definitely triads.

13 (a) **Treble clef:** F major, D major, E minor. (b) **Bass clef:** F major, A minor, C major. As mentioned in the question, it is major IF the middle note is in the major scale of the bottom note. If you listen to these triads, you will hear the difference between major and minor.

14 All triads here have a 3rd and 5th. The first is F major, then C major, then G then E minor.

15 All triads here have a 3rd and 5th. The first is F major, then A minor, then G major then D minor.

16 (a) You see that the first one contains F sharp and the second F natural. (b) You hear the different quality of sound. (c) The first is major. (d) The second is minor.

17 All intervals are a third and fifth. 1 = A minor, 2 = C major, 3 = D minor, 4 = A minor, 5 = E minor, 6 = D minor.

18 (a) true (b) true (c) true.

19 Bassoon, trombone, bass clarinet, tenor saxophone.

20 (a) G major. (b) C = $\frac{4}{4}$ and it indicates four crotchet beats in a bar. (c) Eight. (d) 'Will' in bar 5. (e) The first two and the last two. (f) Two are in bar 6 and the other is over the barline from bar 6 to 7. (g) Bar 6: B to G is a 3rd; A to D is a 5th; D to G is a 4th.

21

22

23 (a) G major. (b) C = $\frac{4}{4}$ and it indicates four crotchet beats in a bar. (c) Eight—the anacrusis is not a bar. (d) 'Leaves', 'grow' and '-in'. (e) a 4th. (f) Bars 6 and 7. (g) There are no tonics in bars 4, 6 and 7.

24 A young swan is called a cygnet in English. (a) G F♯ B E D G A B C E F♯ G A B C D E F♯ B

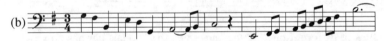

(c) Slur on bars one and two, and three and four. Bar 5 a slur, Bar 6 two slurs. Bar 3 the lower line is a tie connecting two As and the last is also a tie, but you can't tell here because we can't see that it connects to another B.

25 (a) There are three flats in the key signature. (b) B♭ E♭ A♭.

26 Yes, although they are written in different clefs, they sound at the same pitch. One tone above Middle C.

Answers to Unit Seven

1. (a) Near the end of Unit Three, there is an excerpt from a Beethoven *Waltz*, the Queensland version of *Waltzing Matilda* is quoted at various times, *Advance Australia Fair*, *My Bonnie Lies Over the Ocean*, *The Dying Stockman*, Bach's *Cello Suite* in C, Gounod's *Ave Maria*—all in C major.

2.

(b) **Andante** means at an easy walking pace. (c) *Cresc* is short for crescendo and means gradually getting louder. *p* is short for piano and means soft. *pp* is short for pianissimo and means very soft (d) There are two slurs. (e) There is one tie. (f) The rest is a minim rest having a value of two crotchets. (g) *Ave Maria* is a prayer to Virgin Mary. The words of this prayer have been set to music by very many composers.

3.

(b) There are twelve notes with a major and minor Prelude and Fugue on each note. That makes 24 per book.

4. (a) Because it has a key signature of one sharp, F♯, and it finishes on G.

5. (a) The Australian song in E minor we looked at earlier is *The Shearer's Dream*.

7 On a | summer | day in the | month of | May |
   Once a | hobo | was a | hiking |
   Down a | shady | lane thru the | sugar | cane |
   He was | looking | for his | liking. ‖

8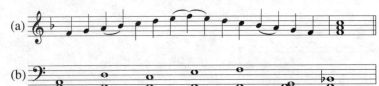

9 (a) A | young man | left his | na tive | town |
   Through | trade be ing | slack at | home |
   To | seek his | for tune | in this | land |
   He | crossed the | bri ny | foam. ‖

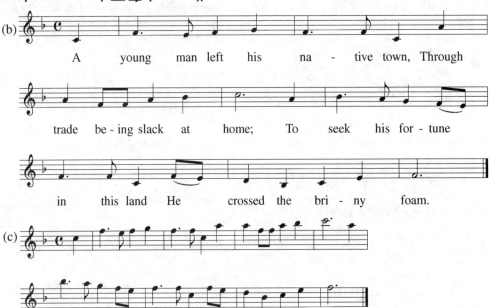

10 (a) Mozart's Oboe Quartet (p. 77) and Bach Minuet in D minor (p. 85).

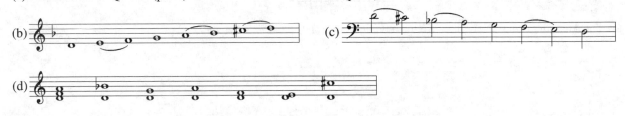

11 (b)

102 Discovering Musicianship Grade One

12
(a)
(b)

13
(a)